FLASHBACKS

THE FLASHBACKS SERIES IS SPONSORED BY THE

EUROPEAN ETHNOLOGICAL RESEARCH CENTRE

CELTIC & SCOTTISH STUDIES

UNIVERSITY OF EDINBURGH

27-29 GEORGE STREET

EDINBURGH EH8 9LD

FLASHBACKS

The Making
of *Am Fasgadh*

An Account of the Origins of the
Highland Folk Museum
by its Founder

Isabel Frances Grant MBE, LLD

in association with
THE EUROPEAN ETHNOLOGICAL RESEARCH CENTRE
AND NMS ENTERPRISES LIMITED – PUBLISHING
NATIONAL MUSEUMS SCOTLAND

GENERAL EDITOR
Alexander Fenton

Published in Great Britain in 2007 by
NMS Enterprises Limited – Publishing
NMS Enterprises Limited
National Museums Scotland
Chambers Street, Edinburgh EH1 1JF

ISBN 978-1-905267-20-0

The right of Patrick Grant to be
identified as the author of this book
has been asserted by him in accordance
with the Copyright, Designs and
Patents Act 1988.

**British Library Cataloguing in
Publication Data**
A catalogue record of this book
is available from the British Library.

Cover design by Mark Blackadder.
Cover photograph: Dr Grant at
Am Fasgadh, Kingussie
(© Highland Folk Museum).
Internal text design by NMSE –
Publishing, NMS Enterprises Limited.
Printed and bound in Great Britain
by Athenaeum Press Ltd, Gateshead,
Tyne & Wear.

For a full listing of related NMS
titles please visit:
www.nms.ac.uk/books

CONTENTS

Acknowledgement 6
List of illustrations 7
Foreword by Hugh Cheape 8

THE MAKING OF *AM FASGADH*

1 Early Influences 11
2 The 1920s 16
3 The Inverness Exhibition 20
4 Iona 28
5 An Historical Outline 45
6 Principles of Collecting 59
7 Collecting in the Islands 67
8 Ardnamurchan, Arisaig and Kyle of Lochalsh 74
9 Applecross and the Sea 80
10 The North-West and Highland Buildings 92
11 West and East 98
12 Perthshire and Angus 102
13 Workers in Wood and Iron 109
14 Other Crafts 119
15 Craftsmen's Tools and Household Plenishings 129
16 Lighting 133
17 Transport 137
18 The Social Pattern 146
19 Laggan 165
20 Kingussie 171

Glossary 192

ACKNOWLEDGEMENT

MANY of the photographs used to illustrate this work were kindly supplied by Lieutenant Colonel Donald Grant and Mr Patrick Grant, nephew and great-nephew respectively of the author. Other photographs used as illustrations were kindly supplied by the Highland Folk Museum, Kingussie. Mr Ian MacKenzie of the School of Scottish Studies Photographic Archive, University of Edinburgh, provided invaluable assistance to the editors by undertaking photography of some of the items used in this work as illustrations. To all of them, and most importantly to Dr Isabel Frances Grant, the editors wish to record their thanks.

Mark A Mulhern, Editor
EUROPEAN ETHNOLOGICAL RESEARCH CENTRE

LIST OF ILLUSTRATIONS

1   Dr Grant aged 4 years, 1891.

2   A somewhat pensive Dr Grant posing for a formal portrait as a young girl.

3   Dr Grant aged 18, on the occasion of being presented at court in 1905.

4   Dr Grant at the Great Sphinx, Giza, Egypt in 1935.

5   The United Free Church in Iona that opened in 1935 as *Am Fasgadh*.

6   Dr Grant with canine companion on Iona with *Am Fasgadh* in the background.

7   Dr Grant showing some of the artefacts *at Am Fasgadh*, Iona.

8   Display of artefacts, *Am Fasgadh*, Iona.

9   Display of powder horns, pictures and other items at *Am Fasgadh*, Iona.

10 Dresser at Iona with Wally dugs.

11 Collection at Iona showing a horse collar, creel, butter churns and buckets.

12 Collection of spinning equipment in *Am Fasgadh*, Iona.

13 Church at Laggan that became the second siting of *Am Fasgadh* in 1938.

14 Dr Grant outside the manse at Laggan.

15 Household utensils in *Am Fasgadh* Highland Museum, Laggan.

16 Pitmain Lodge, Kingussie, the third siting of *Am Fasgadh* from 1944.

17 Dr Grant outside Pitmain Lodge, Kingussie.

18 Display at *Am Fasgadh*, Kingussie showing a range of domestic furniture.

19 Display of kitchen-related items at Kingussie.

20 'General View of Cottages, The Highland Folk Museum, Kingussie.'

21 Collection of buildings at *Am Fasgadh*, Kingussie *c.*1954.

22 Dr Grant on the occasion of receiving an honorary degree in 1948.

23 Field Marshal Sir Patrick Grant, Dr Grant's father.

24 Field Marshal Sir Patrick Grant, Dr Grant's grandfather.

25 Grant family picnic at Balnespick, July 1936.

FOREWORD

ISABEL Grant, known familiarly from childhood as 'Elsie', was first and foremost a Highlander, with a strong sense of belonging in the north country and in particular to the Grant country of Strathspey. She was justifiably proud of her family and their long domicile in the Highlands as the Grants of Tullochgorm, and frequently recalled that both her grandfathers had been Field Marshals.

Elsie was born into the Victorian age, in Edinburgh, on 21 July 1887. As a small child she experienced a long separation from her parents after their posting to India. They had to leave their daughter in the care of one of those illustrious grandfathers, Field Marshal Sir Patrick Grant, Goldstick-in-Waiting to Queen Victoria, and to his daughter, Miss Frances Gough Grant, known to Elsie as 'Aunt Fan'. Her grandfather, who had been born in the eighteenth century, brought close what seemed even then, a distant past. But it was Aunt Fan who nurtured Elsie with visits to the London galleries and museums and laid the foundations of a life-long interest in collecting and in material culture. Later visits to Scandinavian museums, with their emphasis on colourful folk cultures, inspired Elsie Grant to the vision of a museum for the Highlands and Islands which would preserve their vanishing material culture, Gaelic traditions and values.

Elsie Grant's writing career was encouraged by John Maynard Keynes for whom she worked as a researcher. She also fulsomely acknowledged the influence and support of Sheriff J

R N Macphail (1858-1933), particularly in the use and inter-
pretation of Scottish documents. As editor of *The Economic
Journal* from 1912, Keynes published a series of articles by her
and two of the Supplements (1926, 1928) appeared under her
name. This tutoring in social and economic history was applied
to her own people and the Highlands, and exemplified in her
first book, *Every-Day Life on an Old Highland Farm, 1769-
1782* (1924). This analysed in close detail the farm accounts of
William Mackintosh of Balnespick, her great-great-great-grandfather, and described the context, both social and economic, of
Dunachton in Badenoch, an openfield farmtown held in run-rig.
Of particular significance for Scottish history is her sympathetic
evaluation of the benevolent tacksman, a class conventionally
vilified for their perceived role in the decline and collapse of
Gaelic society. Two further major works set the benchmarks for
Elsie Grant's considerable and enduring reputation, *The Social
and Economic Development of Scotland before 1603* (1930),
and *The Lordship of the Isles* (1935), both of which helped to
reposition the Highlands as an object of modern and serious
scholarship.

Travel and research, including cherished and remembered
conversations with an older generation, led to her organising
the 'Highland Exhibition' staged in Inverness in August and
September 1930 when 2,100 artefacts were gathered in for a
'national folk museum'. When this failed to develop, Elsie Grant
used a personal legacy to establish a folk museum herself, opening it in the disused United Free Church in Iona in 1935, and
pursued her self-appointed cause with a steely, often desperate,
determination. This dedication and sense of purpose shines
through in the pages that follow. Later she moved the rapidly
growing collection to Pitmain House in Kingussie where the
Highland Folk Museum opened in 1944 as *Am Fasgadh* ('The
Shelter'). With four reconstructed buildings in the grounds, the
collections of what she always described as 'homely things'
served to illustrate a complex history of farming and fishing,

crofting and domestic life, and their local varieties and regional variations between mainland Scotland and the Hebrides. Her later *Highland Folk Ways* (1961) serves as a 'handbook' to this unique enterprise and her lovingly pursued research and collecting which made it. This current volume is her personal account of the objective that she pursued and the many difficulties that she had to overcome.

The University of Edinburgh awarded Elsie Grant the honorary degree of LLD in 1948 for her creation of *Am Fasgadh,* which was subsequently run by the four Scottish universities from 1954 (when she retired to Edinburgh) until taken over by Highland Region in 1975. She was made MBE in 1959 for her contributions to scholarship and she continued to publish, especially within her own domain of Highland social history and the medieval Lordship of the Isles. Her hospitable Edinburgh house in Heriot Row was a meeting place for scholars, young and old, whom she would entertain at her frequent and congenial soirées. Elsie died in Edinburgh on 19 September 1983 and was buried at Dalarossie in her beloved Strathspey. As author, historian and folk museum pioneer, Elsie Grant was a highly unusual person whose consuming interest in Highland culture and Highland history touched all who met and knew her.

Hugh Cheape, 2007
NATIONAL MUSEUMS SCOTLAND

THE MAKING OF *AM FASGADH*

I

Early Influences

A M *Fasgadh* was the nucleus from which the Highland Folk Museum has grown. It was a pioneering attempt to create a Highland variant of the well-known folk museums of Scandinavia. Visitors to the Highland Museum may be interested to read of the struggle that I had to set it up, of how some of the things were collected, the effect of local conditions upon the kinds of things that the people made and used and, above all, of their social background which was the antithesis of the continental idea of a peasant society. I am writing an informal personal narrative rather than a classified record not only because it seems to suit the informalities and makeshifts of my struggling little museum but because the idea in which Fate so obviously had decided that I was to make that museum, and prepared me for it, is strangely archaic and in keeping with the stock of legends, superstitions and beliefs of the people who made and used the things that I tried so hard to collect. I have not burdened this informal account with references nor would I have quoted them if I had been giving a talk to the people that I showed round *Am Fasgadh*, but most of what I write is based upon statements made in my two books, *Every-Day Life on an Old Highland Farm* and *Highland Folk Ways*, both of which are carefully documented.

My early memories of visits to museums are vivid and happy. I remember that when I was about seven, I was taken to the British Museum and saw the Elgin Marbles, and the feeling of awe, tinged with actual fear, that the sight of that frieze of heroic figures aroused in my mind. Perhaps this childish reaction was more akin to the one that Praxiteles wished to produce in the Ancient Greeks than is that of our modern highly sophisticated aesthetes. Most of my childish memories of museums are upon a less exalted artistic plane and are of many visits to the groups of museums and exhibitions in South Kensington, when my parents used to spend a month or two most winters in London. I like to think that the impressions that the arrangements of the splendid collections that I and my brothers saw as we roamed up and down long corridors helped me long afterwards to make the best disposal that I could of the hoard that I was to accumulate of Highland things.

In the museum containing the Indian and Burmese collections, the glitter and exuberant ornamentation upon the treasures that were upon display rather repelled us but there was a horrid fascination about the implements of execution of the wicked King Thibaw. I felt the 'coming alive' feeling that 'a story' gives to an exhibit. As I was to learn long afterwards, it is the thought of the way of life of the people who had used them that makes one revere the homely plenishings of a folk museum.

Most of our 'afternoons at the museums' and those that we most enjoyed were spent in the Natural History Museum. As active children, we ranged far and wide amid huge skeletons of prehistoric monsters, serried ranks of specimens of fish preserved in glass bottles, animals rare or ferocious that were works of art in the way they were stuffed and in their settings and we learnt to criticise and to appreciate the lay-out of the exhibits. We felt a proprietary pride in a large case showing how some animals grew white fur in winter because some of the familiar animals from home, mountain hares, stoats and weasels, which we called 'our' animals, were prominently displayed there. Long afterwards when I made *Am Fasgadh*, it was for the Highland country people that I made it and to give them a rightful pride in 'feeling their roots'. To be frank, a visit to the National Museum of Antiquities of Scotland, as it was then arranged, produced a very different reaction. One saw large white labels partly masking the exhibits and when one eagerly hoped to gain from them some idea about the exhibits themselves and of the *raison d'être* of their arrangement – which was by no means apparent – all one found was the name of the donor. Rather later on, when I was interested in west Highland carvings, the graveyard effect of the miscellaneously assembled flag-stones was equally daunting. I hasten to add the arrangement of the museum has long since been transformed.

These are all childish recollections. I was seventeen when a visit to a museum had an effect upon me that has profoundly influenced the course of my life. My mother and father had taken me on a trip abroad and we visited Antwerp and went to see the Musée Plantin.

The building had been owned by a famous family of Flemish printers of the seventeenth century. In this old printing works, built round a courtyard with a small formal garden, ancient presses had been set up in their old places and all ready for work, and folios that had actually been printed on them were placed beside them. There was an office with high writing desks furnished with bundles of quill pen and receptacles for sand. But there was nothing counterfeit. There was no gimmickry or, as I always think of them, 'stuffed human beings'.

As we wandered round the old building, a feeling of continuity with the past became more and more potent. It was in a sense a revelation. It has influenced the whole course of my life but only twice have I again experienced it. During the time that I was collecting the homely old Highland things and running the Folk Museum I suppose that I was too much cumbered with the burden of getting the work done and agonising over the problem of how, with my slender private resources, I could meet the pressing demands for expenditure or get through all the work of supervision and maintenance. But once on a misty morning, looking across the field at the Inverness-shire cottage that Mr MacDonald had built, it came over me, and once more after I had given up the museum and was on a trip to Norway, while

visiting Lillehammer, the best sited of all folk museums that I
have visited, I had it again. I hardly dare to wish that *Am
Fasgadh* may have the privilege of imparting such an impression
upon some visitor.

During the following years I led a quiet country life. To have
actual close association with country ways of life is perhaps as
good a preparation for making a Highland Folk Museum as a
purely academic course of study (with its rewarding certificate)
in an English university. I had, moreover, the benefit of my
father's profound knowledge and warm pride in all Highland
things and of his exceedingly acute criticism.

During the First World War, I first did social work in London
and there had a humble post in the Ministry of Labour. I saw
real poverty at first hand and learnt something of office administration and, under a very able chief, of meticulous research.
This way of life, that could have led anywhere, became a direct
but uphill and often stony road towards the making of a folk
museum in the early 1930s. Like everyone who did the sort of
work that I had done during the War, I had read a good deal of
elementary economics and social history. Writers like the
Hammonds and the Webbs abound who describe the life of the
English farm labourer or what they term the 'poorer classes'.
Egged on by Sir Henry Clay, for whom I had done a good deal
of work and learnt a great deal in the process, I had been doing
a little research into early Highland agriculture. Then my uncle,
Colonel George Mackintosh, said I could try and decipher the
writing of a funny old book that he had. It was the account book
of his great-great-grandfather, William Mackintosh, who had
farmed at Dunachton in Badenoch for over 15 years from 1768.
I mastered the faded script. The painstaking record of manifold
details called up vivid images in my mind. The theme of my first
book came into being, and later on all the research and study
that was to go into the making of that book was to stand me in
good stead in the much tougher problem of getting *Am Fasgadh*
onto its feet.

I was still doing the preliminary deciphering of the old account book when I was taken on a cruise to the northern capitals. The ship called at Stockholm, we went to Skansen and I saw my first folk museum. In eager delight I wandered from one to another of the little houses, so skilfully scattered about the uneven ground. They had the same quality as the Scandinavian fairy tales of Hans Christian Andersen. Then I began to notice that among the other visitors that there were a great many who were obviously of the country – some of them real country people – and suddenly I thought, 'Oh! I do wish that there was a Highland Folk Museum for Highland people to see'. It was an idle thought. I did not envisage who was to do the job or still less how it was to be paid for. And yet, stronger than any other memories of the tour – the Viking ships at Oslo, the Rembrandts and Vermeers of Amsterdam, the urban charm of Copenhagen with its rose-red buildings and enticing shops – the memory of this wish remained.

Back at work on my old forebear's account book, I came across terms that were quite unknown to me and also to the local people whom I consulted and they had to be looked up in dictionaries of archaic Scots words. I learnt a method of farming more primitive and toilsome and a way of life infinitely more poverty-stricken than anything my neighbours had ever known. For instance, I learnt that 'tathing' meant driving the grazing livestock every night into a fold that was remade every day in a different place so that eventually another part of the precious 'in-field' was manured by the animals' droppings, or that 'sowens' were made by steeping the husks left after the grain had been ground so as to extract the last vestige of nutriment. This liquid was kept until it had become sour and was said to be a pleasant drink.

2

The 1920s

IN their eagerness to help me, the country-people rummaged in their lofts and outhouses for relics of the past. I was thrilled and delighted when I was shown the first one. It was the iron tip of a cabar lar. I had not done much more collecting before I discovered that, among our bygone Highland things, the iron blades of cabar lars have an exceptionally high survival rate. The cabar lar is, however, an interesting implement. It is made of an oblong piece of iron, two of the corners of which are bent over to hold the end of a curved shaft across the other end of which is a crosspiece. The iron blade, the edge of which has been sharpened, was pushed by main force under a turf or sod so as to raise it. No doubt this implement survived in use for some time because, although it was cumbersome, it was locally made and therefore cheap. It did such work as cutting sods for making a roof or preparing a peat-face for winning the peats, or for work that would have been done much more expeditiously by a spade bought in a shop, but costing more money. In the days of the old unreformed agriculture, the main use of the cabar lar was to skin off the surface of the less good land, to burn it and put the ashes on the land under constant cultivation with oats and barley – the 'in-field', in order to improve the quality of its exhausted soil.

More and more things turned up. My kindly neighbours were amused at my enthusiasm for what they dismissed as 'old troke' and I hailed as deeply interesting treasure trove. They told me what they could about the use of the old implements. But, as I was to find over and over again in collecting, their attitude was an ambivalent one. They had a rightful pride in their race. They could reel off their own family pedigrees and that of their neighbours, but they were reticent about the primitive ways of tilling the land and of living and the poverty of the old Highlanders. I was becoming all too familiar with this attitude when I began to collect further afield and I am proud to know that *Am Fasgadh* did a little to break it down. I gratefully remember the friendship of Annie Noble, Jimmie Dunbar and above all, of Duncan Davidson and much they helped me to understand. With Mr Davidson there was the added link that his ancestor had been a subtenant upon Dunachton when my old forebear was farming it and wrote his account book.

It was bitterly frustrating that though things of great interest and significance were turning up, often in need of some restoration and preservation, and I was learning more and more about them, there was no place they could be looked after and displayed. I must have been an insufferable bore in the way I harped upon the need for the setting up of a Highland Folk Museum before it was too late. I even shocked my mother by incurring the publicity of a letter to the *Scotsman*. The result was nil.

The idea was not only a new one – it was the beginning of a break with a very ancient attitude to the Highlands. In the 1920s a few people were still under the spell that Sir Walter Scott – the Wizard of the North – had cast. A respectable number were conversant with the story of Bonnie Prince Charlie, and some had tackled the works of a group of outstanding historians – Sir James G Fraser, W F Skene, P F Tytler, A Carmichael and others whose work on the Highlands had been published by this time. A great many more had enjoyed such novels as *Catriona* and D K Broster's *The Gleam in the North*. But it was not then widely understood that the essential fact of old Highland society was that society, of all ranks, was of aristocratic origin and not peasant, and therefore was the antithesis of that of Norway which is now so widely accepted as the basis for folk studies.

This fundamental difference was brought home to me when, in the 1920s, I was working upon another book, *The Social and Economic Development of Scotland Before 1603*, and the evolution of the clans was a specially congenial study, tracing their development down the centuries and the growth of their political power. Furthermore, older relations still kept up the ancient Highland pastime of retailing and swapping genealogies. When these could be carried far enough back or if contemporary accounts survived, they gave a personal knowledge of how the social fabric of the clans was built up. It consisted of many layers or strata closely associated by the link of a family feeling – ties of kindred is too exact and cold a phrase to describe the warm emotion of a feeling that did not always rest upon actual genetic fact (the ancestors of some of the most devoted clansmen had originally adhered to and been adopted into the clans). In passing, I may note that I was glad to point out in that book that the old system of agriculture, so primitive and inferior to later methods, was originally Scots and common to the whole country, not specifically Highland, although it is true many of the deprived districts in which it lingered the longest were actually within the area of the Highlands.

During this time of frustration of all of my efforts to get anything done about the making of a folk museum, I became aware of a new fact in the old life of the Highlands. The work of the Abbey Theatre in Dublin was in the full flush of its early success and a season at the Court Theatre in London was a major theatrical event. I saw a performance of 'Deirdre of the Sorrows' by Synge. I was profoundly moved by the heart-rending story and the utter sincerity of the actors. I had had a vague idea that such a story, along with tales about Finn and his comrades, had been told in the Highlands but recollection of them had been lost by the Highland folk I knew. I now read the early version of the epics, alas only in translation, and was again profoundly moved. In my adult mind there was a tinge of that childish wonder which the Elgin Marbles had once produced in me. They belonged to a world almost as remote as fairyland and yet the people in them were so intensely human. With a few possibly older tales they are in two distinct groups – the Ultonian Cycle which contained the splendid exploits of Cuchulain and the moving tragedy of Deirdre, and in the Fenian Cycle the mass of tales about Finn MacCoul and his band of warriors.

These epics the Highland people so constantly repeated that they became literally localised in the Highlands. The Traighmor in Islay became the scene of a great battle; Finn's murder of Diarmid, an episode in the Feinne Cycle, was localised at Ben Gulabin in Perthshire; the place where Deirdre made her home in the Highlands was located both on Loch Etive and at Inverfarigaig on Loch Ness. General David Stewart (writing in the early nineteenth century) described how in Perthshire a stranger on visiting a township was hailed with an eager enquiry if he had something to tell of the Feinne. In spite of constant repetition, the stories in the two Cycles were never mixed up and the well-defined characters of each of Finn's hunter warriors were always kept distinct.

To me, the old Highland things I was so anxious to preserve had never been quaint and amusing oddities, but the setting to the daily lives of people of my own stock. When I realised that the recitation of these magnificent epics along with music, song and improvised verse had also been part of the people's everyday lives, I felt a new regard for them. I could never hope for anything more rewarding than to create a museum adequately preserving the setting of the past life of the stock of which I am sprung – the people of the Highlands.

About eight years passed. I continued, quite fruitlessly, to try to find someone who, somehow, would establish a Highland Folk Museum and for all that time I knew that the precious old things that I wanted to save were mouldering away in some loft or being thrown out or destroyed as 'rubbish and troke'. And then my luck seemed to turn. Fate was giving me another shove towards the job I was to do.

3

The Inverness Exhibition

AT long length, in 1930, I was able to interest someone far more influential than myself in the need for a Highland Folk Museum, Sir Alexander MacEwen, a Highlander born and bred. As Chairman of the Education Committee of Inverness County Council and a leading solicitor in Inverness he was exceptionally well informed in Highland affairs. He had been elected Provost of Inverness. I had the sudden happy idea that a Highland Exhibition at Inverness might lead to the setting up of a folk museum. I suggested the plan to him and with his influential backing it came off. He and Dr Evan Barron became joint chairmen. A committee of the leading personalities of the north was formed. Mr Athole Mackintosh and Mr R R MacEwen were appointed joint secretaries and I advisory secretary. The Highland Exhibition was opened in the Inverness Town Hall on 4th August 1930 and remained in being until September 20th.

Inverness Town Hall was an ideal place for this purpose. It is large and central and it has two of the pictures that I particularly wanted to show – an early one of a man in Highland dress and a portrait of Joseph Mitchell who did so much for the roads and railways to Inverness.

The Exhibition tried to illustrate as wide a range as possible of all the aspects of Highland life: history and prehistory; agriculture; crafts; household plenishings; weapons; heraldry (for which the future Lord Lyon, Sir Thomas Innes of Learney, made a beautiful set of shields emblazoned with the arms of the principle clans); fishing; sport; and transport.

Dr A O Curle, Director of the Royal Scottish Museum in Edinburgh, who had given me a great deal of advice and encouragement, came to see the Exhibition. To my relief he thoroughly approved of the set up. Its successful start was largely due to Charles Iain Fraser of Reelig. He was the perfect colleague in the enterprise. At that time he was still very young but, with his family connections, he knew Highland society from top to bottom and he also knew where the treasures that we most wanted to exhibit were to be found. He had the charm and tact in which I am so sadly lacking and he worked like a beaver.

My chief activity before the Exhibition had been the collecting of the homelier exhibits (a good many of which eventually found a permanent home in *Am Fasgadh*). In the future, after the museum had taken form, I was to take many, many collecting trips much further afield but they were to be among strangers and to take place when I was hampered by financial limitations and other cares. My happiest memories are of those early trips. I had in mind the things that I had been shown when I was working upon the old farming diary and wherever I went I got a warm welcome, but there were a few disappointments. There was a sad tale of a flail. It had been discovered when things in a loft had been routed through to find something for me when I was hunting out the meaning of old words. But instead of being returned to peaceful obscurity, someone had suggested that it would be handy for beating carpets. Unfortunately, at the first blow the swingle pole had been shattered. But there were happier incidents. I remembered seeing a cradle that had rocked generations of babies in the owner's family. When I asked for the loan of it, she shamefacedly admitted that the previous winter it had been broken up for firewood. She was a little taken aback by the heat of my reproaches and promised that her husband would go to get a cradle that 'was the very spit of it' that she knew of further up the Strath. It was fetched and just in the nick of time, for the man who had it had just been about to saw it in half to make a hen-coup. The chalk mark along which he was going to saw it was still on the floorboards. That cradle safely ended up at *Am Fasgadh* chalk mark and all.

Collecting rather further from home at the upper end of the Strath, Kathleen MacKenzie of Glen Kyllachy was a staunch ally. She was upon terms of the closest friendship with the people there and in the scattered group of small houses known as 'the Coigs'. Our visits to Mrs Beaton in her lovely little house – the finest example I ever saw of the old local Strathdearn type of house – and her welcome and generosity are specially happy memories.

A friend of Kathleen, Princess Dhulip Singh, often came with us and was very popular with the people that we visited. One especially good day stays in my mind. We had espied through a window a muckle-wheel, an early and simple type of spinning wheel, amid the lumber of a deserted house. We arranged for its safe transport. We acquired other treasure such as a crois iarna for winding wool into skeins and a 'cheeser' (for pressing cheeses) in a most dilapidated condition. Unfortunately, while we were so engaged, my little dog had been searching for what were antiques in her own estimation. She had found some horror and had rolled in it. On the return journey, my small car contained besides myself as the driver, Kathleen, who fortunately was slim, the Indian princess who was rather plump, our various finds, my small dog and a very, very large smell.

Upon another occasion I was told that if I went to a certain place I would find the pot and an illicit still. Of course, I hurried there. It was a beautiful specimen, a vessel of hammered metal about three feet wide. With exultation and joy I managed to get it into the car, took it home and proudly telephoned to my chairman, Alec MacEwen, of our acquisition. To my dismay he replied that it was illegal to possess such a thing and that I must return it at once. I pleaded that as a lawyer he could surely find a way round the law, but he was adamant. The road had been quite empty when I had driven home with the pot sitting in my open car. On the return journey the pot was muffled in rugs and I met about every soul I knew in the Strath, including the local bobby, on the way. I felt rather envious when, about 30 years later, I visited a folk museum in Skye and saw the reproduction of a complete still.

Mr Mackintosh, our honorary secretary, had recruited a team of assistants, mostly students on vacation, to help in arranging the exhibits and then to look after them but, of course, I spent most of my time at the Exhibition. One learnt a lot from the comments of knowledgeable visitors. There was the touching incident of an old man who had spent most of his life overseas and had come back to find that all his family and neighbours were dead or gone and the ways of life in his old township quite changed and who returned again and again to linger over the homely utensils and plenishings that reminded him of those of his childhood. During the years that I was to have my own folk museum and was showing people round the same sort of thing happened many times over. On the other hand another visitor, looking at our collection of milk cogs – of which we were rather proud for milk cogs are made of staves of wood that shrink if the cog is allowed to dry out and then the whole thing falls to pieces, old cogs therefore are not easily come by – exclaimed scornfully, 'When I was a boy in Strathnaegow, such things were as common as blackberries'. As his hair was snow-white and he had obviously seen out a good many winters, I doubted if they were still as common in Strathnaegow.

Very mindful of the frustration I had felt on visiting certain museums and with memories of happier visits in my childhood, I was very keen to supplement the exhibits with written matter, such as the songs, stories, *etc*, that were associated with them. I was rather proud of this innovation. We had the snuffbox belonging to a certain Captain Macpherson, a notoriously bad character known as the 'Black Officer'. He had gone for a New Year's carouse in the Forest of Gaik and an avalanche had swept away the hut in which he was staying, but, according to the local tale, he was carried off by the Devil. I duly had all this recorded upon a card beside the snuffbox until a furious lady complained that I was miscalling her ancestor and I had to take it away. Nevertheless, except for this episode, the written matter was much appreciated. I carried on having it at *Am Fasgadh*.

One of our greatest embarrassments was when we were offered exhibits that their owners thought were genuine antiques with historical associations and which were probably of a later period of manufacture – Charles Iain Fraser with his exquisite tact and very sound practical knowledge dealt superbly with these awkward incidents. One of mine was when Wendy Wood, a well-known character, who claimed psychic gifts and wished to 'scry' (crystal gaze) into a charm stone that was one of our greatest treasures. The Exhibition was crowded and I did not want to open the case in which it was kept. Still less did I want to risk censure by members of the Free Church for allowing the exhibition to be used for such heathen-like practice. She was a very forceful and persistent lady. She declared that she had obtained the permission of the owner to 'scry' into the stone. I replied that it was at that moment in our custody and that we were responsible for its safety. My refusals became increasingly acidulated. She announced, 'I shall go and ask your Chairman'. I rushed to the telephone and told Alec that a very angry lady was coming to see him but that her anger would be nothing to my fury if he let her have the crystal. He coped and not only did she not return but sometime afterwards, when we happened to meet in Edinburgh, she apologised for her unreasonable demands.

It was a great delight to me that, especially on market days, numbers of country people visited the Exhibition. It was, of course, to help towards founding a museum especially for them that I had started the idea of the Exhibition. Other visitors in great variety came to see it. I think that our most distinguished one was the Prime Minister, Ramsay MacDonald. The Duchess of Sutherland brought him. She was interested in everything and well informed. She had herself done a great deal of work for the Highland Home Industries. He was mainly interested in the Jacobite relics. I think that they were about the best looking pair among all our visitors.

The Exhibition itself was quite a success but the effects were evanescent and did not achieve the object I had hoped for. No movement to establish a permanent Highland Folk Museum resulted. I myself gained much experience and information on many subjects. I wrote to the people who had lent me things suitable for a folk museum when years later I had a place to house them and had a generous response. I managed thus to salvage a certain amount of extremely useful material for a future museum. And I kept the set of shields with the armorial bearings of the clans that Sir Thomas Innes had painted for me. When at last I did have a museum, it gave me great pleasure to set the shield bearing the arms of the ancient Lord of the Isles in the place of honour directly over the doorway. Besides being most decorative, these shields emphasised the high descent of the Highland people and emphasised the non-folksy aspect of the collection.

An even more valuable acquisition was a set of cards with samples of wool dyed with vegetable dyes and with watercolours of the plants that were used. The woollen samples had been given to the Exhibition by Miss Helma MacCallum, the lady who managed the Highland Home Industries shop at Strathpeffer, and the illustrations were made by the staff and pupils of Inverness Academy. This collection had aroused great interest while it was in the Exhibition and it was to prove one of the major attractions when I was able to display it in my museum.

We had been able to show a much wider variety of farm implements than those I had met with in the high uplands of Strathdearn. I realised that there was more and more to learn about and to try to preserve. A treasure that was probably unique was a great eight-oxen plough from Cradlehall used in the rich farmlands near Inverness. It had been a thrill to see the monster being carried up the staircase of the Town House. The driver of the lorry that had brought it had had to enlist the help of some of the men who invariably used to stand about the square outside the Town House. In the rural economy of Scotland (apart from much of the Highlands where the soil was lighter and a four-horse plough was used) the layout of the farms was adjusted to the capacity of these ox-ploughs. They normally consisted of a 'plough-gate' divided into eight 'ox-gates', each of which was expected to supply an ox for the team of the common plough. A photograph of this plough was taken but we did not carefully record its dimensions or the details of its construction. It was years before I had any place at all in which to preserve the old implements and by then it was too late, as the plough had been destroyed. It is still more regrettable that no other means of saving it was available. Fortunately a great many other exhibits did eventually find shelter in *Am Fasgadh* at Iona and went on to Kingussie.

The Inverness Exhibition gave me a most valuable education in the finer Highland antiquities, the treasures locked away in the chests of old Highland families. So far, I had been concerned with the sort of things that are chucked into a loft or shed on the chance that they might be useful some day. Among the treasures in the Exhibition, apart from some carved handles of dirks and quaichs with interlaced patterns, the style of the silverware was that current in its period and much of it was actually imported. It was the evidence that such exhibits furnished of different grades of society living in different ways and yet closely related that was so interesting. Of even greater interest were the examples of ancient Highland textiles. Besides their intrinsic beauty, the subtle blending of their colours and the intricacy of their patterns expressed something of the individuality of the people who wove and wore them.

Because of these loaned treasures the Inverness Exhibition, although it was transient and makeshift, did represent the old Highland way of life in a manner and a degree that I could never hope to achieve again. The dress, the highly stylised music, the complex metres of the verse, the austerity of the epic tales were common to everyone in a many-sided society. They were aristocratic. I was going to found a folk museum that has survived, but try as I have, it would be an illusion to imagine that I was ever able to put across even the faintest simulacrum of old life in the Highlands.

4

Iona

IT was disappointing that, the Exhibition having failed to develop into something more permanent, I was to make no progress towards getting a folk museum set up for five more years. The Exhibition formed a basis for talks about what should be done. With more definite prospects of something it was rather a shock to meet with not merely the former indifference but an attitude of disapproval from some of the Highland people whose opinion I most respected. They felt it was undesirable to record the poverty and the primitive way of life of earlier times. For instance, a lady whom I very much revered and who had a great influence, refused for this reason to try to preserve a particularly attractive little house near her home. One at least of my closest relatives had this feeling. I was to meet it again and again among the folk that I met when I was collecting and it gives one a feeling of satisfaction to know that the modest amount of esteem *Am Fasgadh* enjoyed has done much to modify this attitude. Nevertheless at a time of frustration it was bitterly wounding and discouraging.

One rather odd little incident happened soon after I got back to Edinburgh. I had to go to a bazaar and thought that the best way of spending my pittance was to take refuge in the fortune-teller's booth. She studied the lines of my hand in the usual way and made the safe and conventional remarks of her trade – that something good was likely to happen in the near future – that when I was not being nice, I might have a temper and so on. Then, suddenly, her voice changed. She began to gaze intently into the palm of my hand. This was interesting because in a very old description of a Skye fortune-teller he is said to have read hands not from the lines like a modern palmist but by gazing into a drop of ink in the palm of the hand. She said that she was puzzled and added, 'You're not particularly fond of children are you?' I agreed emphatically. She said, 'I thought not, but I see some little houses in your hand and I thought you might be going to be a house-mother in one of the little separate houses some children's homes have'. The interview closed. I am pretty sure she cannot have known about me and my plans for a museum and as a matter of fact I had not then realised the need for several cottages. But at that precise moment Fate was arranging that I should learn of it.

It happened that soon afterwards Dr Curle, in course of conversation, asked me if I had a clue to the fact that a certain style of pattern was only to be found on the grave slabs and other stone carvings within a well-defined area of the western Highlands and Islands and that they all belonged to a distinct period. After a great deal of thought I came to the conclusion that the area and the period roughly corresponded with that of the rise and dominance of the great Lordship of the Isles. I became fascinated by the idea of the great semi-independent principality and of the Gaelic way of life within it. I would have loved to have tried to write a history of it but there did not seem to be enough suitable written sources to furnish more than the barest narrative. I therefore decided to write an account of the areas that had once owed allegiance to the Lord of the Isles and to indicate the vestiges that remained of the influence of the old Gaelic Principality upon them. So I embarked upon my book, *The Lordship of the Isles*. Of course, in order to write it I had to do a lot of travelling within the lands of this old lordship. In doing so I learnt two very important things. Firstly I learnt of the whereabouts of a number of settlements of old houses, the very places where one might hope to find the material suitable for a folk museum. Secondly, for the first time I discovered that there were several distinct types of cottage building in the Highlands, each one especially suited to conditions and materials locally available. I was, of course, familiar with the type indigenous to Strathdearn and much of the central Highlands. The country is well wooded and the local stones are knobbly and not very tractable for building. Therefore the most essential parts of the building are the 'couples', pairs of cabers (originally small tree-trunks) set like inverted 'V's to carry the main weight of the roof. Now I saw for the first time the houses of the wind-swept treeless Outer Isles with dry-stone walls to withstand the western gales and support roofs built with the minimum of timber. In the south west, where the stone is laminated and there is fine timber, more spacious houses of quite a different shape were built. There were, of course, many more local variations.

One became rather an expert in recognising the different types. For instance, I was travelling on one of McCallum, Orme & Co's cargo ships and we put in at Talisker in Skye to take on a cargo of whisky. I was told that I could walk by a road over the hills to the next port of call at the end of the next sea loch. I came to a newly made crofter settlement. All the houses were newly built with ready-made materials in the usual Board of Agriculture style, but the outhouses, made by the crofters themselves, were in the Harris style. A man working by the road greeted me and was greatly intrigued to find out how I possibly could have known that the community had actually lately been settled from that island.

My travels made me realise how much wider the scope of a Highland Folk Museum would have to be with all these different types of buildings to illustrate but also how much more important the need for it was becoming. In the early 1930s the Scottish Board of Agriculture was carrying on a housing drive. Every steamer that I travelled in appeared to be loaded with piles of window frames, sanitary equipment, *etc*, and they seemed to be piled higher upon every pier at which the steamer called. One began to wonder if any cottage of the traditional type would be left.

At the same time I had become very much interested in amateur drama and was the producer in a very small group of amateurs. One learnt a good deal about the importance of lighting and colours and of the balanced setting of the scenes and about the gentle art of camouflage that was a good preparation for displaying my exhibits to the best effect when the time came.

I little knew it but the time had almost come. In 1935 I began to feel restless and disorientated. Some of my best friends were leaving or had left Edinburgh. Mr Rappalovich, the kind host whose home had been a powerhouse of stimulating ideas, had died. My contact with a small group of amateur actors came to an end. I let my flat. I went south to seek pastures new but did not find them. I was preparing to go to visit my brother and sister-in-law in Egypt when it happened that an acquaintance who had been staying on Iona called. I had been there in the course of writing *The Lordship of the Isles*, so we naturally compared notes. She remembered the Free Church had been closed and was for sale and she thought that it was going cheap. I had a little cash in hand from the sale of some of my furniture. Suddenly I was struck not by a mere idea but by a resolution. I would buy the church. I would make it into the Highland Folk Museum. I would, as my mind literally phrased it, 'do the blasted job myself'.

I wrote in haste to my lawyer desiring him to buy the church. I got a most diplomatic reply asking for clarification and obviously really inquiring had I quite gone out of my mind! I wired emphatic instructions and caught the boat for Port Said. I received a cable that the building was mine. I felt rather pleased with myself. I little thought of the length and hardness of the row that had to be hoed before it was to become a museum.

As soon as I arrived back from Egypt I went to Iona to inspect my new possession and to arrange for my own accommodation.

On one of my former visits to Iona I had peeped inside. A large deal pulpit and an array of deal pews had filled the interior and it had seemed quite small. Now, all the furnishings had been taken out and I have the most vivid memory of how vastly different the floor space seemed to stretch before me and the gaunt walls to loom above me and how, I wondered, how ever, ever, ever was I going to fill the gaping void. The answer began to come on my way from that brief visit to stay with my mother in Strathdearn. I was worrying about how to get enough exhibits when I remembered how kind Mr Wolfenden, the proprietor of the Gordon Arms Hotel at Kingussie, had been in lending exhibits from his collection of homely Highland things to the Exhibition at Inverness and I wondered if he would lend me some with which to make a start. I thought that I would write to him and ask him as I did not know him personally. But as I passed through Kingussie and glanced at the hotel I thought that there was something unusual about the look of it. I generally did not stop more often than I could when on long drives but propelled by impulse I got out of the car to investigate. I learnt that Mr Wolfenden had sold the hotel and that the new proprietor, Mr Stewart, had arranged for an auction of most of the contents to be held the next day. He was obviously extremely busy but I buttonholed him and asked him what had happened to Mr Wolfenden's collection. He was vague but pointed to a pile of miscellaneous objects and said that if the auctioneer thought it worthwhile anything there would be put up for sale next day. I looked at the pile and saw aged stuffed stags' heads that had for years decorated the walls of the hotel, meat covers battered by long service in the kitchen and similar objects but, sticking out, was the shaft of a peat spade. I was allowed to look through the pile and picked out various ancient implements. I offered to buy them but Mr Stewart said he did not know what they were worth and that they would go into the auction. I said, 'Give you ten pounds for the lot' and the deal was done. We put the things into a lock-up garage because, as soon as I had been seen to pay money for them, other people became interested in them too. Next day, I borrowed my brother's larger car and fetched them. I little knew that years later they would come back to Kingussie.

In Strathdearn, willing hands gave me back all that I had borrowed for the Exhibition and more articles that had been routed out during the intervening years. I had kept note of the other exhibits that I would hope some day to house and display and I wrote to all their owners and met with a very generous response. I did not go back to Iona empty-handed.

The immediate problem arose of what to call the museum. I was quite aware of some of the limitations. The church had only a few roods of land around it. One could never hope to build even one cottage let alone all the types of Highland cottages. I just hoped that some time and somewhere such a museum would eventualise and being then entirely ignorant of the hierarchical attitude of officialdom, I imagined that I would have some part to play in it. In the meantime, I felt that in the desperate need for searching out and rescuing the vanishing relics of our past, the new museum would be invaluable as a place where they could be kept and cared for. I decided to call it *Am Fasgadh* – The Shelter. My friends will think it characteristic of me that when this great idea came to me I spelt the word wrongly. The Rev. Donald MacCuish, my first visitor, who became a valued friend to the museum and to me, rectified this with exquisite Highland tact and a strong sense of fun.

Inflation has so much changed the value of money that it may be worth recording that at this time my entire income amounted to under £400 per annum. In the money value of those days an income like this enabled me to live in the way usual for single women in my position. I had a flat and kept one maid. I was able to keep a small car. These arrangements had to be changed. My flat was let, as at that moment the market for the sale of such flats was poor. I spent a good deal of the year living on the cheap and making short collecting trips on the mainland. The summer I spent looking after the museum and showing the collection, and boarding in a farmhouse or small hotel. In the late spring I always made a collecting trip to some less accessible area. The trips that I had taken when working on *The Lordship of the Isles* stood me in good stead in knowing where to go.

My first job was to arrange for some simple supports for the display of my collection. When enquiring I was told that there was a carpenter and joiner upon the island. I hurried off to see him and met one of the kindest of friends and a staunch supporter of *Am Fasgadh*, Mr MacCormick and his wife. He could turn his hands to anything. He gave unstinted help with a cheerful friendliness to *Am Fasgadh*. His wife laid out and tended the beautiful garden in the ruins of the nunnery. Our friendship extended to our dogs, my cairn and his fox terrier. I hope that the collection still contains a gift that Mr MacCormick made to it of a 'cuman' or water-carrier. Such cumans were used before tin pails. They are very scarce. All vessels made of staves are liable to dry out and their large size made them specially liable to breakage. I had set my heart on getting one and had failed when the MacCormicks went to spend a day on Coll they said that they would bring one back for me. They were as surprised as I was that they actually did so.

Iona did not have for me the strong attraction it has for some people. It has a few lovely little bays (one saw watercolour sketches of them, the best by 'Bunty' Cadell, in every exhibition of pictures that one visited in Edinburgh). When one went to them they were always occupied by at least two groups of picnickers with portable gramophones in full blast. But Iona shared with many other Hebridean islands, spells of light and colour when the white sand took on an incandescent brilliance and everything else a celestial purity of colour, although it did not have the miles and miles of that shining sand found along the western seaboard of the Long Island. The real truth is that living on a small island that was also a tourist centre was distasteful to me.

Iona is the most sacred and historic site in the Highlands. I had already visited it twice to study and examine its buildings and wonderful store of carvings. The visits had partaken more of educational exercises than of pilgrimages, nevertheless one had been well aware that one was treading upon ground that had been holy to untold numbers of people before one, generation after generation down the centuries.

To me, one great attraction of a stay upon Iona was its wild flowers. On my collecting trips I never stayed long enough in one place to see the whole sequence of this blossoming. Iona is especially rich in its flora and several very rare species grow there. One visitor, an ardent botanist, found one. I forget its name but the flower was very small, greenish in colour and not at all pretty. She was a little crestfallen to find that it was the very profusion that delighted most of us – the matted clumps of small tenacious plants that stippled the brows of the cliffs with colour, the gay yellow flowers that flaunted themselves in the fields (where they should not have been at all), the drifts of colour that filled every waste spot and feathered the sides of the roads and tracks with an infinite variety of form and hue. Their glory was already fading when the September gales brought the pageantry of summer to an end.

The people of Iona that I had contact with were friendly but I always felt that they classed me among the summer visitors and did not realise my Highland origins. Then, almost at the end of my stay, an old man who had often stopped to pass the time of day with me, called to say goodbye. He remarked that he had come to realise that I really was Highland. I asked him what had made him aware of that obvious fact and he replied that I thought a great many things that I did not say 'and every one of them uncomplimentary'. I hope that I have not written too many of them down.

Some of the visitors really loved Iona and went back to it again and again. Others, one felt, would have been happier at Rothesay or Blackpool. Mr and Mrs Russ and their daughter

Louise became faithful friends to the museum and to me. He was a chartered accountant and with professional skill he made out a balance sheet and initiated me into the keeping of accounts by double entry. The family of the great Norman MacLeod of Morven kept in close touch with the island. An unusual group was a family of tinkers who travelled from island to island in their own boat and had a hen that roosted on the top of their tent. One daughter was in service in Cadogan Square, London.

A studious-looking lad, after hunting about among the shingle in the bay to the east of the museum, came to ask for a little box in which to put some eoliths that he had found. The shores of Iona are particularly rich in pretty, water-borne pebbles. But as the bays where one finds them are bounded by rocky headlands and high seas swirl around them, some of the pebbles get chipped. I thought that this was what had happened to the boy's pebbles and wooden boxes are very precious upon Iona for use as kindlings because twigs and branches are very, very scarce. The boxes and crates in which new exhibits for the museum sometimes arrived were far more desirable in the eyes of the local people than were their contents. Nevertheless the lad was so delighted with his finds that I parted with a little box. He said that the next day he was going to examine the bay on the west side of the museum where there was a larger bar of shingle. He came back next evening. His pockets, hat and hands were full of stones and he eagerly exhibited them and asked for a larger box, which I gave him. He said that next day he was going to the end of the island to Port-na-Curaich. The bay there is completely covered in shingle. I thought if he were able to transport his finds he would need a packing case. He was pale and slight and I wondered if he could carry such a load. He never came back. He did not perish from exhaustion by the way, for no corpse was found. Someone must have convinced him of the bitter truth.

Iona was apt to be visited by people with unconventional views about the arcane. One lady, who happened to be staying at the same boarding house, had irritated me by again and again bringing in wild flowers of the same kind, asking their names and then dropping them to die. A friend, a social worker named Marjory, one of whose professional assets was a most sympathetic manner, was spending her summer holiday with me. After a little chat, the lady said to Marjory if she promised not to tell anyone (meaning me) she would take her to see something wonderful. Of course, Marjory went and with them a band of kindred spirits. They crossed the open stretch of land in the middle of the island to a small field and the lady pointed to a circle of grass near the gate. 'A fairy ring', she said in an awed voice. Marjory was just thinking that the Little Folk must have had remarkably heavy feet when a man came out of the farmhouse close by, went straight to the ring and pulled a tethering pin from the middle of it. Seeing the watching group he remarked that 'Yon calf had made a fair mess of the grass'. It appeared he had sold the calf and had tethered it there for its new owner to fetch it. In silence the group broke up. The grassy country was open and they made their separate ways back to the boarding house.

I cannot resist recalling one more memory of Iona. In those 'pre-War' days it was rather dashing for women to don slacks. A few would-be dashers so attired were waiting to be taken on one of the cruises round the island run by a local man. As they giggled with such male friends as they had made, a girl in a grey skirt came down to the jetty, stepped into a dinghy moored there, put out to sea, raised a mast, hoisted a sail and was off and away as quietly and as naturally as a sea-bird takes wing. Meanwhile the dashing young women were being handed onto the motor boat like a group of sheep. I felt proud that I knew that girl.

During my second season at Iona I had an extremely disappointing experience. I had become more and more anxious that the existence of the museum should become widely known because so often people had said to me that they had had this and that of the very things that I wanted to save and that they had 'let the children play with them', not knowing what to do with them, or had disposed of them in some similarly disastrous way. For the museum's sake I did want publicity. When I heard that a team from the BBC was coming to do some recordings on Iona, I was full of high hopes. They came. They gave full coverage to the Iona Community as was to be expected and they filled the rest of their programme with hackneyed island subjects such as fishing, which is of minimal importance upon Iona, and they ignored the first folk museum to be set up in Scotland. That particular broadcast was widely listened to and some people who knew of the museum thought poorly of it because the museum was not mentioned. The BBC did the cause of the conservation of our Highland heritage a very ill turn.

During my third season upon Iona the museum received a pleasant piece of recognition. A British Empire Exhibition was held in Bellahouston Park in Glasgow and I was asked to arrange a little Highland 'roomie' in the Historical Pavilion. I supplied plans. The surface of dry-stone dyking was cast in plaster and most realistically coloured. The roof was of real peat. The electric fire that glowed under the peats in the middle of the floor looked real! I was delighted when I arrived and helped to put the finishing touches. Things were at the last stage of preparation and there was rather a hold up of the erection of barriers at the doors of the various rooms. Some of them were to illustrate a very grand way of life back to the eighteenth century and were to contain valuable furniture. In the erection of the barriers the humble little 'roomie' seemed to be of small consideration till the foreman actually in charge of the joiners declared roundly, 'I'm from Argyll myself and I'll NOT see the Highland room treated as second to any of them'.

Secure in this knowledge and awaiting delivery of my own crates of things, I was able to have a prowl round the pavilion and admire its beautiful contents at close hand and chat with the people who were in charge of them. It was interesting to watch Dr Meikle, at one time Librarian to the Advocate's

Library (now embodied in the National Library of Scotland) arranging a display. He had models made of wood or cardboard the exact size of his treasured volumes when shut and open and he was carefully placing these models, moving them about and contemplating the effect of his arrangements from some feet away. He was obviously enjoying what he was doing. I could not linger, the packing cases of my things had been brought to the 'roomie'. I took out their contents and the cases and packing cases were taken away. I was hastily putting the exhibits – which were lying about all over the floor – into the places that I had planned for them in my own mind when I heard voices. I looked round – watching me from the doorway was a group of the 'High Heid Yins' who had arranged the other rooms. I heard someone say 'crowded' and was relieved when he was asked by someone else if he had ever seen a little old cottage that wasn't crowded. The subject of crowding when displaying everyday things is an important one that I shall hope to return to.

That Highland 'roomie' was a success. Louise Russ, who kept a kindly eye on it, said that, especially in the evening, people, evidently retired from the Highlands to Glasgow, used to visit it and would recognise the sort of bowl or cogg that they had seen their mother using. One night my friend was horrified to see a mouse running among the things and as she was thinking to herself that next day she would report it to the authorities, she heard someone say, 'Just look, there's a wee mousie – they think of everything!'

It was towards the end of my time upon Iona that I received a most generous gift for the museum from the people of Iona. The pulpit and seating arrangements in the parish church were unusual. The pulpit was placed in the middle of one of the side walls instead of at the end of the church with all the pews arranged to face the minister. The pulpit was a two-tier struc-ture to accommodate both the minister and the precentor. I had admired it and when I heard that the arrangements in the church were to be changed and the pulpit replaced, I was very anxious that it should be preserved and great was my joy when the upper part of this interesting pulpit was given to the museum. It was a really generous gift because wood is precious on Iona and the pulpit was large and made of very good timber. It was also a timely gift. Long afterwards it was discovered that the pulpit was one of the few surviving examples of the interior fittings of the churches designed, or at least approved by Telford, the great engineer.

By the second season I had begun to realise that I would have to find more extensive premises for the collection. It had grown apace. At the end of the first season I calculated that I had about 2,000 exhibits, which had already been arranged right round the walls and I had had to have a series of compartments of hessian nailed onto a light wooden frame set up down the middle. By the end of the second season these were becoming well filled. Of course, I had also displayed pictures and written material, anything relevant that I could get hold of. A friend had managed to obtain a card with a reproduction of a few sentences said to have actually been written by Saint Columba. Before I labelled it a visitor, who said he was a graphologist, looked at it and remarked that he had never seen a handwriting that showed such a tremendous force of character but he added that it also revealed a pretty hot temper. Saint Adamnan's life of the Saint does not belie this.

I could not enlarge the church because the building covered nearly the whole of the small peninsula upon which it was built. A secondary building would have been difficult to run and I do not think that I could have got the land or been able to afford to pay for it. In any case I knew that the island was not the right place for a general Highland Folk Museum. For one thing it was too definitely Hebridean. Of much greater importance was the difficulty of access to it. This was the cardinal objection. It was in an isolated, out of the way corner off the main lines of travel. It would never be easily accessible to a wide range of visitors. And, to be honest, I did not want to make the sacrifice of immersing myself for long periods so far from my friends and other interests. When the summer season steamer service was not running, to get to Edinburgh, one had to rise at cock-crow, walk to the ferry to Mull (which was an open boat) and cross that island by bus. At Craignure, in those days, the steamer lay off the shore and one had to go out to her in an open boat. From Oban the connection by train was good. One arrived about mid-day and if the start had been wet, one found the white sand of Iona still clinging to one's shoes. I remember one most embarrassing journey to Edinburgh. My little dog, Vari, was in season. A large proportion of the canine population of Iona accompanied us to the ferry and some members of it even swam after us. Dogs seemed to spring out of the ground at Fionphort and Craignure and I longed to reach the steamer. It happened, however, that there was a sale of sheep on at Oban and the steamer was full of shepherds, every one of them with at least one dog – some with two. Vari and I spent the voyage in the 'Ladies'! The difficulty of access was an insuperable bar to the visits of all but a few holidaymakers.

The difficulty of getting to Iona, however, was really a stroke of luck for me. Because of it, I often had the pleasure of staying at Dunollie. Mrs MacDougall of MacDougall's warm love of Highland things was an unusually wide one. She could appreciate and show her appreciation of other people who worked for the Highlands and sometimes were ploughing rather stiff and lonely furrows. For instance, she welcomed to her home Miss Francis Tolmie, the collector of Highland songs, and Miss M E M Donaldson, who wrote such racy accounts of her rambles in the Highlands. To me, she gave the warmest encouragement. She even came with me on a collecting trip – but that requires special mention. To stay at Dunollie itself in some of my comings and goings from Iona was a great treat. It is the family home of the Chief of the MacDougalls, the oldest clan in the Highlands. The place was full of associations with a long and honourable past. Its greatest treasure was the Brooch of Lorn but my fancy was specially taken by the targes. After the Disarming Act had been passed they had been used as covers for the butter kegs but they are now framed and hung on walls of the hall. There was a hospitable, home-like feel about the house and about the welcome one got from the family. It was the same sort of welcome that one got in the homes of people of real old Highland stock whatever their circumstances, down to the poorest little cottage. I wish, oh how I wish, that one could convey something of that background of good breeding to the homely plenishings one shows in a Highland Folk Museum.

The difficulty in transport also was a great drawback in getting exhibits to the museum. I did not attempt to acquire and transport the great ox-plough that we had borrowed for the Exhibition in Inverness. Realising now, and too late, how unique it was, I do most deeply regret this. It was often difficult to get things properly packed and crated and the cost of the transportation was a consideration. Too often people were inclined to tie an addressed label to some fragile old thing and consign it to the mercies of road, rail, steamer and ferry. If one were bringing stuff with one, fellow passengers would often lend a hand. On one wet and chilly voyage from Oban I remember how one kind fellow traveller produced a large mackintosh and I thought he was about to put it round my shivering shoulders and thanked him warmly. Instead, he draped it round the handle of an old wooden racan – the handle of an aged peat spade that had lain about uncared for through years and years of Highland weather.

There were still no signs of anything being done to create a Highland Folk Museum so at the end of the second season on Iona, I started to look for a place that I could afford to continue to run on my own that was accessible and otherwise suitable. I cannot now exactly remember which places I looked at at this stage and which I visited a few years later on. Some I looked at upon each occasion. But it was certainly at this time that I went to Ullapool to look at a little water-driven wool-mill that had been closed. I had rather wanted to have this building because these small mills, driven by water power and weaving the traditional country-made cloth, were an interesting development from the older, domestic, hand-weaving industry. To buy it, however, was not a possible proposition. In wandering around it, I had espied a bobbin winder. It looked like a simple kind of spinning wheel. I bought it and took it back to Iona. When the museum opened next summer, a visitor, an elderly man who looked quite obviously in comfortable circumstances, was clearly delighted to see it. He told me that he was the son of a weaver and in the further chat he said that he remembered that a usual punishment for weaver's children was to make them wind a number of bobbins. He turned the wheel gently with his hand and said, 'and what a number of bobbins I wound!'

I was also very much drawn to the idea of trying to find a site for the museum at Oban. I realised that this would be very much a west coast site for a Highland museum but Oban has been termed the Charing Cross of the North. I already had friends who would give invaluable support and the country was congenial to me. I saw two admirable sites but could not possibly afford to build and the feus and rates would be high. There was no available empty building and I am sure that, if there had been, it would have been too expensive. While in Iona, I also prospected round Tobermory. I had friends nearby at Aros and I very much liked the country. There was a minute glen that would have been an ideal setting. But Tobermory was about as inaccessible as Iona and the expense of building and fencing would have been prohibitive. In the end I heard of a large empty church with its manse at Laggan in Badenoch that could be leased and I decided to move my collection there. It was just as well I felt an urgency to move, because about eighteen months ahead war would be declared and Iona would be for years within a Prohibited Area. I made arrangements for my collection to be moved and to sell the church in the autumn of 1938. The little church itself I had grown fond of. The building was absolutely plain and very well proportioned and it was an amusing hobby to plan what a delightful home it would make.

I had arranged for a removal firm to pack the exhibits. The men that they sent were excellent. By early October everything was crated or securely bundled together and carried down to the jetty to wait the coming of the cargo ship to which they would be taken by boat. Then gale after gale blew up. Atlantic rollers surged through the Sound. No sail could call. The stuff lay by the pier. I spent a miserable and frustrating time. At last, in early December, the ship was able to lie off the jetty and the stuff was rapidly got onboard. She was not to go directly to Oban so that I was able to go overland to Laggan to open the church and be ready to receive the collection. There had been a fall of snow. The roads were extremely slippery. The temperature inside the church was literally glacial. I planned where I would have the stuff dumped. As the day wore on I remembered all the awkward corners where on these icy roads the pantechnicon could have skidded and overturned. I got colder and colder and the early dusk fell. Finally by the light of the motor lamps the things were carried in. By now speechless, I went to Newtonmore, to Main's Hotel where Miss Main had lighted a roaring fire in my room, and she sent me straight to bed and kept me there for the inside of a week.

5
An Historical Outline

THE houses and exhibits that are preserved in a folk museum did not come from a static society. It greatly adds to one's interest in them if one knows a little about their historical background. For the benefit of people who are not familiar with Highland economic and agricultural history, and with great trepidation, I have ventured to make a brief and generalised summary of it.

Anyone who visits the west coast of the Highland mainland must be struck by the belt of brownish golden seaweed that fringes the shore. If one knows other parts of the Highlands, the difference in the lay-out of the agricultural land comparing much of the mainland on the one hand with the north and west coast and the Western Isles on the other, appears to be equally striking. It takes, however, a good deal of reading to realise the connection between the two. It was even more striking in my young days before the agricultural depression, mechanisation and the attractions of wider opportunities overseas and in the towns had taken their toll and in consequence a great deal of land had ceased to be tilled. Most of the cultivated land in the Highlands is covered by a beautiful pattern made up of rectangular fields which run at different angles according to the contours of the hilly slopes, their colours varying in accordance with the rotation of the crops that they bear – barley, turnips, hay, pasture, oats – according to the season – dark earth, green light and dark, and most beautiful of all – golden at harvest time. Set at commanding points in this pattern of fields are the houses

45

of the farmers so that each one of them can keep an eye on his crops and stock. They were, and still largely are, plain, four-square little masonry buildings, slated and with their chimneys in the gable ends. They are period pieces of the Agricultural Revolution and quite different from the traditional local type of houses. In the north western Highlands and Islands, although some of the land is cultivated in this way, the general pattern is of organised groups with strips of land under the different crops of the rotation. The lay-out varies according to the lie of the land, but a common arrangement is for houses to be dotted at intervals along the road and with strips of land under different crops that belong to an individual crofter to form a complete block in a long stretch of cultivated land.

I did not attempt to do so, but I think that in the ideal Highland Folk Museum, large-scale views of those contrasting types of the layout of the land should be shown – perhaps as murals. There should also be reproductions of estate maps or reconstructions based upon them that would illustrate the kind of agriculture that preceded these layouts. Apart from dairying and textiles and some furniture, most of the objects that one tried to collect dated back to the period before the Agricultural Revolution. Now that things are changing so quickly, I think that the maker of a folk museum would be faced by great difficulty in deciding what to collect. There was a definite post-Agricultural Revolution and pre-First World War period in the Highlands but already during its course practically everything that the people used was imported and not distinctively Highland.

Under the old system, the arable land was divided into 'in-field land' – which was the best and most accessible and which was kept under a succession of cereal crops consisting of 'black oats' (and inferior variety), barley, bere (an inferior barley) and rye – and 'out-field land'. This consisted of the less good, less accessible land – often of natural patches, often of ground on the rougher hillsides. A portion of this land was kept under cereal crops without any fertiliser for year after year until it was so exhausted that it was not worth cultivating. Then it was left to recover and another bit of the out-field was brought under cultivation. As Adam Smith pointed out, this method of husbandry resembled that of primitive people just emerging from the hunting stage of civilisation. The care of the in-field was only one stage better. All the available manure was put on it but the effect of constant cereal crops was never modified by a fallow nor was any better provision made for the winter-feeding of livestock.

The in-field was unfenced (as was the out-field) and, by constant ploughing with old-fashioned wooden ploughs (such as that which figured in the Inverness Exhibition), was worked into high ridges. To work these clumsy ploughs and their team of animals and for all the other primitive methods of husbandry, such as reaping with the sickle, a great deal of human labour was required and so cultivation was generally done by a group of joint tenants or of joint sub-tenants of a tacksman (literally a tack, *ie* lease holder, but in the Highlands generally applied to a larger farmer). To ensure equal effort by, and as far as possible equal results for, the joint cultivators, their individual shares in the jointly held farm were divided up among the rigs and thus the term 'run-rig' came into use.

It is fascinating to try to reconstruct in one's mind's eye what the well-known landscape of upland farms looked like before the reforms. Apart from Slezer's there are no pictures of the countryside like the enchanting views in the background of Italian Old Masters, to my undevout mind often the most attractive bit of the painting. There are, however, a number of estate maps. Those of the estates forfeited in the Jacobite Risings give most extended views and there are written reports, county by county, to the Board of Agriculture, besides many travellers' descriptions. In the wider Straths one pictures the in-field of the different farms as a succession of patches of cultivation upon the lower slopes of the hills and the out-field as lesser spots among

47

the dark rocks, heather and woodland of the rougher ground. But, and this is of great importance, the bottom of the Straths, what is now the most fertile land was nearly all marshy swamps and there were dark boggy patches in the cultivated land because there was no field drainage. This great improvement was brought sharply to my mind when I was working on my book *In the Tracks of Montrose* and learned that the course of the battles both at Auldearn and Kilsyth was greatly affected by the swampy state of ground that is now perfectly sound farm land. I know of land that can now be cultivated by tractor and that all my life I have thought of as ordinary farm land but it is full of primitive field drains and must once have been a swamp. I would dearly like to show a picture of one of these early field drains made of stones picked off the land and built into a channel at the bottom of a tranch in the folk museum of my dreams.

Under the old methods of agriculture the people were subsistence farmers – they actually lived upon what they grew. Their main, often their only, source of money was from the sale of their cattle, the trade in which had developed after the Union of the Crowns in 1603. Young stock, in good condition from the summer grazing, generally at the sheilings, was driven – and ferried and swum where necessary – from the Highlands and Islands to a central tryst at Creiff or Falkirk and there sold to English dealers for fattening in England. It was the first organised industry in the Highlands, the local lesser gentry being involved in its organisation, and it is typical of the state of the Highland society in the seventeenth and early eighteenth century that cattle reiving became an equally important occupation and one that seems to have been more prestigious. 'Coll of the Cows' – MacDonald of Keppoch – was only one of the lairds who indulged in it. Traditions of the drove roads and trysts were still quite strong when I was collecting. The museum of my dreams would certainly have a map of them and also some of the silver buttons that the Highland drovers who took the cattle into England are said to have worn as a means for paying for their seemly burial if they should unfortunately die on the road. I tried hard to obtain such a button but never even got on the track of one. I am also disappointed that I have never been able to unravel the history of Highland cattle. The only description given of them is that they were black, a colour never found in the modern Highland breed. It is possible that they were more like Galloways. Another possible explanation is that because they were rough and shaggy the term was applied to them just as it used to be to the older cottages with dry-stone walls in contra-distinction to the more modern, mason-built cottages.

The division of the joint farms into separate holdings, the more extensive plans for field-drainage, in many cases the building of separate farm houses that replaced the cluster of the dwellings of the joint tenants were all the work of the land-owners. During the middle and later part of the eighteenth century there was a closely-knit group of important improving landlords. In the Highlands the two outstanding representatives were the Duke of Argyll and the Laird of Grant. There were also a number of lesser ones including MacDougall of MacDougall. Their example was gradually followed by other landowners and not only was a large proportion of the existing agricultural land brought under the improved methods of cultivation but, when the price of grain rocketed during the years of the Continental Wars, a good deal more was added by intakes of less suitable land as well as by field drainage.

A folk museum can only try to indicate the vast changes in the ways of life of the country people that the Agricultural Revolution brought about – from a condition of extreme poverty, utterly dependent upon the cruel variation of an unpredictable climate, yet with standards of behaviour that we look back on with envious admiration. In collecting their implements of husbandry we can show change from locally made wooden implements with the minimum of iron reinforcements to imported implements, mainly of iron and steel, and the transition from the great ox-drawn plough to the gradually improved form of the two-horse plough. In dealing with the agricultural implements, craftsmen's tools and domestic plenishings, one noticed again and again that in fertile districts iron was much more freely used than where the land was poor and that the introduction of the use of cast iron and steel made a dramatic change in agricultural practices and in the fabric and plenishings of the houses. I occasionally saw primitive tools such as the cabar lar and the peat spade in use, but everywhere, except for one exceptional farm in Wester Ross, the old run-rig system of agriculture had been replaced by more modern methods. All the same one noticed traces of the older method in the ridges of the old rigs still visible under heather or grass where land had gone out of cultivation.

The size of individual holdings varied from district to district, even from time to time. A very careful student, Marshall, working in Perthshire, put the average at about five acres of infield, four of out-field, with common shares of peat, wood and pasture. In addition, besides the joint tenants upon a farm there were generally a few lesser workers or cottars who worked for a rig or so of land and pasture for their beasts. On the comparatively fertile land of a farm in Badenoch cultivated by a forebear of my own in the 1760s, upon an averagely good year – and I stress the word 'good' – the yield of the sub-tenants' holdings averaged about 17 bolls of grain a year. Sir John Sinclair, a well-known authority on social conditions in the Highlands at that time, put the average consumption of a man at 6 bolls, of a woman at 4 and of a child at 1. Of course, in addition the family had to find what modicum of food they could spare for their livestock – the work beasts, the cattle which not only supplied the dairy products which formed an important element in their diet but also the bullocks, the sale of which was their main source of money, and also the sheep, valuable for milk as well as for wool, and the goats. They had to find money for rent, for some other expenses such as the minister's stipend and for such necessities as they could not themselves manufacture. English visitors who penetrated to the Highlands in the eighteenth century, although they were used to the very low standards of living of the English farm labourer, all commented upon the poverty of the Highlanders. It is very easy to imagine that the standard of feeding of the sub-tenants and still more of the lesser folk was very low. Sinclair gives an estimate of their diet, which entirely consisted of cereals of their own growing, of potatoes and of the dairy produce of their cows. He adds that 'not five pounds of meat was consumed by the entire family throughout the year and that an egg was a luxury'. He was, of course, writing about the late eighteenth century when potatoes were beginning to be widely cultivated and were becoming the mainstay of the poor. Other accounts corroborate Sinclair's more detailed summary, especially in regard to the lack of meat in the lesser people's diet.

The food supply of the Highlanders was in general not only meagre but also uncertain. The lie of the land affected it and worse still the vagaries of the climate. On the west, the Atlantic brought the benign influence of the Gulf Stream but also incessant gales and clouds that discharged themselves in rain as they were driven against the barrier of the Highland hills. Most of the mainland was above a level conducive to successful husbandry. I personally have spent much time in Strathdearn, the upper valley of the Findhorn. It is just over 1,000 feet above sea level. I had, however, friends and relatives who lived close to the Moray coast, near Nairn, not 20 miles away as the crow flies although much further by road and with a long pull uphill. On the same day I have seen the harvest already reaped near the coast and the corn still green in Strathdearn and equally in the spring, very important in an economy that largely depends upon stock-raising, I saw the fields vividly green with the spring grass and still aridly bare in the hill country. Nor is the weather dependable. The figures of yield that I quoted were averages. The climate was so uncertain that harvest, especially on high ground, varied from year to year. I have the permission of George Dixon, who has made a study of the subject, to quote his conclusion that, very generally, on an average, there was a really bad harvest every five years or so. Such a harvest might involve the disastrous necessity of using the corn set aside for the following year's seed for food. Writing in a materialistic age when circumstances and environment are allowed to condition our standards of conduct, to me the extreme poverty of my people is a matter of pride and not of shame, because in the words of the French traveller, Simond, 'they had a superiority to want'. They were no starveling peasant race but proud and brave and courteous. They had high standards of performance in their intricate forms of music and verse and yet also men and women sang as they worked to rhythms that put spirit into their labours and, when they chose, they could improvise. Their splendid epics they preserved not in folios only available to academics but by constant repetition.

The eighteenth century also saw the beginning of the systematic development of road transport in the Highlands. It is typical of the conditions of the country that when the government, who were alarmed by the Jacobite menace, made a beginning and appointed General Wade to build a system of military roads in the 1720s, the General should have written to Mackintosh in a very conciliatory way to ask him to forbid his people from interfering with the working parties of troops. He probably wrote in a similar way to other chiefs through whose land the road went.

By the second half of the century masonry bridges were being made on roads that were being greatly improved. This required the presence of craftsmen and the distribution of their wares. The improvement in agriculture could hardly have taken place without adequate transport. It is important to note that much of the maintenance of the roads was done by local labour supervised by members of the local lesser gentry.

The eighteenth century was an era of tremendous enterprise in England and southern Scotland. It was the time of the Industrial Revolution. Attempts were made to discover and develop mineral resources in the Highlands – iron, copper and coal with minimal effect. A lumber industry developed in the great forests of Strathspey and Rannoch and forestry has continued to be carried on in the Highlands.

The spinning of flax into linen yarn, organised with government aid, became quite an important rural industry. Hitherto women in the Highlands had only spun with the spindle and distaff. Spinning schools were set up to teach the women to use the muckle wheel (an older and simpler kind of spinning wheel in which the wheel is turned by hand) and the more familiar spinning wheel that is worked by a treadle. One is apt to think of the spinning wheel with its fitful cadence as the epitome of olde worldliness and it was already well known in the Lowlands, but such was its unromantic entry upon the Highland scene. The rural linen spinning industry died out later as the use of cotton fabrics supplanted that of linen and a method of spinning linen yarn by machinery (more difficult than the spinning of cotton) was invented.

I rather stress the poor returns of agriculture and the poverty of the people because unfortunately it was a dominating fact in their lives. During the later part of the eighteenth century and the early part of the nineteenth, this archaic system was almost entirely swept away, but the process was gradual and patchy. For instance, in Strathdearn one farm was winning a prize for growing turnips – still an exciting new crop – long before another just across the river was still under primitive run-rig. Generally, the change was systematically carried out by the landowner. The farms were divided and the rigs were levelled, the cluster of joint-tenants' cottages being replaced by small separate farm houses strategically placed to oversee the land of the farms that formed such a characteristic pattern in the lay-out of the greater part of the Highlands during the nineteenth century.

Unfortunately two developments had a very adverse effect upon the Highlands. The first of the catastrophic developments that vitiated the progress of the great agricultural reforms was brought about by a change in the local breed of sheep. The old Highland sheep were small and had very fine wool. They were housed during the winter and were largely used for their milk. Their wool was for domestic use and not for sale. Specimens of the breed are said to have survived, especially on St Kilda. I tried, but should have tried even harder, to obtain a few of the animals themselves or at least good photographs of them. I think that it is most regrettable that the breed was not perpetuated upon St Kilda. Instead, some sheep from the neighbouring island of Soay were taken there and allowed to interbreed with the native stock. The Soay sheep are totally different in appearance and so a breed of sheep of great importance in Highland history had been allowed to vanish without even a pictorial record. About the middle of the eighteenth century, according to traditional history, a careless individual farmer left some of the hardy Linton or black-faced sheep out all winter on the hills. They survived. It was an age when contact with their equals in the south was making the Highland gentry most acutely aware of their poverty and when the rents due to most of them were heavily in arrears, when the beginning of the Industrial Revolution was whipping up economic enterprise in a feverish crescendo and when the coarse wool of the black-faced sheep had a good market. Lowland farmers realised that profit could be derived from the bare Highland hills and offered tempting rates. The tragedy was that the ewes and lambs required better wintering on the sheltered lower ground where the people lived and grew their daily sustenance. 'The Clearances' followed. There are contemporary accounts and modern writers have tended to dramatise the worst events in a sordid, most deeply regrettable phase of Highland history. As one travels about the country it is a pitiful sight to see the patches of land that had been worked up into rigs still clearly traceable under the heather and grass – though not all result from 'The Clearances', and to my knowledge some of the derelict land that I have seen was voluntarily given up when the people decided to seek a better life overseas. In conversation with people when I was showing them round the museum I was often struck by the strong feelings that the 'The Clearances' arouse even in people otherwise not much interested in Highland social history. Often I was tempted to put people's moral indignation down to the fact that most of us enjoy having a good 'hate' upon aesthetic or idealistic grounds. In making this record I look forward to indulging myself in one of my own at a further point in my odyssey. Too often it is assumed that all the derelict arable land in the Highlands was cleared for sheep farming. This is not the case. The demand for the coarse black-faced wool dwindled as finer wools came into good supply and a number of the sheep-farmers went out of business. Meanwhile, the general agricultural depression was affecting the upland Highland farmers more and more severely and with closer contact with the rest of the world the prospects of greater amenities and better opportunities elsewhere brightened. I would venture that through intake and field drainage more land has been brought under cultivation during the past 250 years than has been deliberately cleared for sheep and that by and large and allowing for exceptions, of which I admit that there are probably a number, where the derelict land shows evidence of having been levelled, drained or divided into fields it was not cleared for sheep farming or to the advantage of the proprietors, but owing to the Agricultural Revolution.

The hardy little black-faced sheep, 'a stylish kind of sheep' as one book describes them, were the principal cause of the clearings but they have also become the mainstay of the upland Highland farmer. The appearance of the breed is changing. Their faces are spotted instead of coal-black and the muzzle is not so long and narrow. I used to think that the ends of their fleeces floated about them like a Victorian lady's petticoats when she was seen in déshabillé, so elegantly befrilled and flounced were they. In the Folk Museum there would certainly be a place for pictures of this breed, which has played so vitally important a part in Highland history.

The second development that marred the changes brought about by the Agricultural Revolution has left problems that are still with us. It was brought about by that luxuriant growth of tangle on the shores of the western coast – the 'Golden Fringe' as for only too short a time it came to be called. The wars upon the Continent had entered their final phase in the struggle against Napoleon's domination. As a shrewd blow at the 'nation of shop-keepers', he had laid an embargo upon trade with Britain. In retaliation, the British Parliament prohibited foreign imports, among them barilla, a chemical that came from Spain and was a valuable agent in bleaching of linen and the manufacture of soap and glass. In the enterprising spirit so characteristic of the age it was quickly realised that alkali derived from the burnt kelp formed a possible alternative to barilla and the idea was quickly taken up by the owners of suitable seashores in the western Highlands, the Hebrides and Orkney. A certain amount of labour was needed to gather the kelp and to burn it in kilns. I am ashamed that I did not investigate further and try to find the ruins of such a kiln. I did, however, secure a 'kelping iron', a long iron rod upon a wooden handle that was used to stir the decomposing kelp. People were encouraged to settle by the shore to gather and prepare the kelp. It was part-time work and they were accommodated with small pieces of land for their partial support. There was an extensive shift of population. When peace was declared the duty on barilla was removed. The manufacturers preferred it to kelp and the industry collapsed. The result was disastrous for kelp workers who were crowded upon holdings insufficient to maintain them. The situation was made worse because some of the people who had been displaced in the clearing for sheep farming also settled in these overcrowded communities. The introduction of potato growing, which had reached the islands about the middle of the eighteenth century, made it possible for a greater concentration of people to exist upon the land. These conditions continued for over half a century.

Until the 1880s in Britain as a whole, the Highlands formed only part of a more general interest chiefly focused upon Ireland. It was the Gladstonian era and I remember that as a child staying in London with my grandparents I heard the slogan, 'Three acres and a cow'. Conditions in the Highlands were described by the Napier Commission of 1883, which had been appointed because of a growing public unease, and action was no doubt stimulated by the lowering of the franchise in an act of 1884. About the same time there was actual unrest in a few areas and the repressive measures that had had to be taken were extremely unpopular. In 1886 the Crofters' Holdings Act was passed. This act embodied principles of land tenure that at that time were revolutionary. To avoid technicalities and details – within the crofting counties, Argyll, Inverness-shire, Ross and Cromarty and Sutherland, as well as certain areas outwith these counties – the new act applied to any parish where rights of common pasture existed for which payment was less than £30 a year, and a tenant was enabled to become a crofter with security of tenure, the right of compensation for improvements and the fixing of a fair rent. A number of further enactments were made in the following years (for a good summary see A Collier's *The Crofting Problem*) to maintain a system that was increasingly becoming archaic. Nearly all my collecting trips were undertaken within the crofting areas of the west and north, surviving as they did mainly because of all their special state aid. They formed a splendid collecting ground for me, but as I was only a transient visitor I did not then realise the great social change that had taken place in those areas as a uniform population of crofters had replaced the variety in people's possessions and social background that had always characterised the Highlands.

It was a courageous attempt to relieve the distress of a most unfortunate area, but conditions had changed and have continued to change. The depression in agriculture, the change from subsistence to commercial farming (which rendered accessibility to markets essential), the introduction of scientific improvements and of mechanisation, which have affected the farmers of the rest of Scotland, have also been felt by the crofting communities and more and more effort has had to be made by the state to subsidise them.

This long disquisition is meant to explain the different conditions in the districts that I selected as the most suitable places for collecting. One can write it down. The reader may wisely decide to skip it. But can the great changes be indicated in a folk museum? The Scandinavian open-air folk museums when I saw them seemed to represent a static state of society that has never existed in the Highlands. In the Highlands I feel that any attempt to preserve the setting of life in the past ought to take into account those well-marked periods into which it falls. It was, of course, quite beyond my limited individual attempt to do so.

6

Principles of Collecting

THE story of the making of the Folk Museum changed its course when, in 1938, I moved to what I hoped would be more permanent quarters at Laggan. The coming of the Second World War in the following year was to affect the scope of my work still more. Although I did not realise it, the days of my most active collecting were over, though I was to go on learning more and more about the social conditions that had brought about the material setting that I was so anxious to reproduce and, of course, in every kind of way that I could I went on adding to the collection.

The principles upon which I tried to collect were easy to define. How I was actually to get the material for my collection was a difficult problem. It was in no sense a commercial transaction. The things that I wanted to obtain had generally been discarded by their owners or were decrepit and outmoded. To know what to pay for such things was often difficult. From visits to junk-shops and scrap-yards one got ideas. To country people far from shops, a small gift was often more welcome than money. They were generous in giving me things that they had no use for. Only once in all my collecting was I asked a fancy price for an article. It was for a cruisie and I had seen them for sale at a cheaper price in Lady Lawson Street (a great haunt for antique dealers) in Edinburgh. Generally, the people had forgotten that they had the very things that I wanted or thought little of them and did not realise their interest. For instance, when I stayed with Mrs Macdonald at Rudhanan Gadheil, near Lochmaddy, she was very popular and she had broadcast to her many friends and acquaintances that I was coming and was collecting old things. A message came back that a woman at (I think) Salen, a hamlet along the road, had something very old that she would let me have. We went along in 'Alecky' – Alec's tin lizzie, a car that he drove where I can imagine no other could manage to go. To my chagrin the very 'old thing' was an aged sewing machine. It had been set on the table in the parlour and its kind would-be donor was disappointed when I said it was not what I wanted. I helped to carry it back to the outhouse where she had kept it and there, relegated as useless, was one of the things that I very much wanted, it was called a 'larder' – a sort of cupboard with an opening in front protected by vertical wooden bars. To digress a little – in the course of my collecting word was several times given me of interesting old things which turned out to be such outlandish objects as a Ghurka Kukri, a Chinese lucky mascot, or a cup made of half a coconut. Long afterwards, I happened to be comparing notes with the curator of the Folk Museum at Cambridge and she said that she had never been offered similar things. Such relics have their own significance as the possessions of a race that has ventured over the wide world but it would be misleading to display them in a Highland museum.

In collecting, I was to discover that some people were not only indifferent to relics of the past, but were ashamed of having them. I have no doubt that their feeling was derived from the days when children were beaten for speaking Gaelic in school and when Highlanders were despised by the Lowlanders for their poverty and different way of life. For instance, a very kindly man who had directed me on my way and had listened sympathetically to my account of what I was trying to do, said that he had a few old things that he had found in his house. He mentioned a goffering iron, then he became more and more embarrassed. Then he said he had something else that he would really not like to show to a lady like me. I pressed him, and he became increasingly unwilling to show it to me. As a well-brought-up spinster, I began to wonder what kind of object of depravity I would be shown. At last, he produced something about which I had read and had longed to possess. In the old days in districts where the cattle and people were housed under one roof, when the potatoes had been boiled for a meal in the big pot hung over the fire, a flat wooden platter with a wicker-work edge was put upon a sheaf of straw and the pot was tipped to pour the potatoes and water onto it. The ring of wickerwork allowed the water in which the potatoes had been boiled, and which had a modicum of nutriment, to run onto the straw which was then given to some cow that needed special attention. It had come down from times when the family lived in a more primitive way. With real generosity he let me have it.

I feel sure that behind a feeling of embarrassment over the possession of things from a more primitive past, lay some ancient taboo about the disposal of goods belonging to the dead. The people had so little regard for their old possessions that sometimes they threw away quite saleable articles upon the rubbish dump. A spinning wheel was once recovered for me from such a place. At the same time a most interesting example of the lack of possessions from imports and of the ingenuity of the people was brought to me. It was a bit of broken looking-glass fitted into a home-made wooden frame.

When one realised that people had such feelings one felt that in approaching them one was committing an act of intolerable intrusion. Fortunately practically everywhere I went I was fortunate enough to meet with at least one kindred spirit who welcomed the idea behind my collecting and not only used their influence but took time and trouble to go with me upon my visits and who incidentally taught me a great deal. Among a great many of such helpers, I specially remember the district nurse at Tarbert; a man who walked round Bernera with me; and the tenant of a lovely old house at Laide.

I had always assumed that one would get most things from

old houses and out of the way houses. This often was not so. When people were rehoused fifty or more years ago it was not so easy to buy things and they were more inclined to put things that were broken, or that they did not immediately need, in a barn outside 'as they might come in handy some day'. In out of the way places rehousing often came much later and this did not happen. I remember a trip on Loch Etive in the little steamer that plied up and down it. I had thought that at the head of the loch I might find treasure trove. It was a lovely sail. The shore was rich with associations. Deirdre made her refuge here when she fled to Alba. At Ardchattan was the old Premonstratensian monastery. I had visited the old churchyard there to see the carved gravestones, wonderful in their variety and quality, a flowering of Gaelic art. I enjoyed the rich historical associations on the sail but I did not get a single thing for the museum for the houses in the little settlement at the end of the loch were all fairly newly built.

People ask me if I enjoyed collecting. The plain answer is 'No!' I am shy and lacking in self-confidence and social address. It was agony to approach a hamlet and to feel critical eyes were looking out from behind the curtains of every window and that their owners were all asking, 'Whoever is this woman and what is she coming here for?' Invariably, I was courteously received. The coming of a stranger was a pleasant event and I felt that my coming was welcome but there was always the worry of how far I could pry, how much ought I to offer, how much could I afford and how on earth I could transport anything I did get.

I am also often asked if I did not find that not being able to speak Gaelic was a great disadvantage. I do not think that it was. Nearly all Gaelic-speaking Highlanders are now also bilingual. They are extremely proud, sensitive and shrewd. They might resent it if one opened the conversation in Gaelic although, no doubt, some would warm to it in further talk. I am a poor linguist. Abroad foreigners receive one's efforts to 'rub along' with amusement. It would be fatal to try to do it in Gaelic.

Nevertheless, it is sometimes useful to know a word or two. I once heard someone in the background say in Gaelic that only a fool would be trying to buy the things that I was trying to get. I quickly said 'chan'eil' – 'No', and in the shamed consternation that followed I could have demanded and got everything in the cottage. I think that it is a more valuable asset to have a country background – not merely not to commit the solecism of leaving gates open or walking on growing crops but to be able to show a knowledgeable interest in how the crops were faring in the vagaries of the weather, to be tactful in not taking up the people's time at seasons when they are specially busy as for instance when they are making their hay, which is a process that can drag wearisomely in the west, to be able to comment appreciatively upon any good points in the livestock or crops. Above everything else the most valuable thing that a collector can have is a contact – a mutual friend or even a far more remote connection with someone known to the other party. It was of great advantage to me that my brother had been adjutant to the Lovat Scouts for some years. I was also lucky in having friends as friends of friends, who lived at various strategic points in my wanderings.

Because Highland country people are very sensitive and exceedingly good at 'putting two and two together' and because in remote places, memories and traditions last longer than in towns, I have been careful not to tell any anecdotes that would hurt anyone's feelings if the place where it happened could be identified. The story that gives me the greatest pleasure to recall is a case in point. I was leaving one place for another. As usual, I was short of cash and thought that I would keep what I had and take the afternoon off and go up the hill to see the view. As I was setting out a woman who had been kind and helpful met me and told me of three more families that she thought might be worth visiting. As she had been so kind I reluctantly decided to visit one of the houses. When I got there I was taken into a room that showed great poverty and a girl looking wretchedly ill was lying upon a bed in the corner. The woman of the house had set out what she hoped to sell me. I chose a couple of things and the price that she asked was a good deal more than I was prepared to pay. She was, however, so desperately anxious to sell them that I agreed to give the price. She was delighted. She volunteered to carry the things to the house where I was staying and I went on for my walk. On the way back I met my helpful friend. The woman had told her of my call. She told her she was desperate to get money to buy proper food for her daughter who had diabetes (this, of course, was years before the Welfare State), that she had been upon her knees praying for help when I walked in and bought what she thought was old rubbish. In some of the bad patches that the museum had to live through, I liked to recall the memory of that visit.

The most touching response to my efforts to collect and preserve came soon after I had moved to Kingussie. A friend living near Forres told me of a man who collected old things and we went to visit him. He said that he had worked on farms but he had a very nice home and garden. His collection was a very varied one. He was interested in hearing of the museum, and sold me some trifles. About two years later I received a message that he was dying and would like to give the museum anything that I thought was of value as his collection would be broken up. I went to see him. He was laid up but his wife showed me round and kept urging me to take all that I wanted. I took some nice and unusual things. I was deeply touched and grateful and most anxious to do some little thing to show my appreciation but his wife was insistent that I was not to send fruit or papers or anything, as they wanted the things to be a gift with no return. I racked my brains and had an idea and as soon as I got back to Kingussie hurried to see Mr Ian Johnstone, the editor of the Badenoch Record, a local paper that was read from cover to cover by everyone in the district. He was co-operative. The next issue contained a special article upon the valuable gift that the museum had received. A copy straight off the press was sent to the dying donor. It reached him in time.

I do not enjoy roughing it, am not of an adventurous disposition, was not in my first youth or a good walker, and travel was less easy even fifty years ago. Roads and ferries were not good. It was not easy to tranship a car to the islands and the air service was only just beginning. I was hampered at every turn by lack of finance. I tried very hard to obtain a grant of some kind but nothing was available. When I think of what could have been done in those days with the facilities that are now available when it is almost too late I feel disgusted.

Once, in Mull, I came across a very primitive old cottage standing derelict. I was sure that its contents were equally ancient. Neighbours told me that the owner had died in Glasgow and that his heirs did not live in the district and that they were going to dispose of the holding and were coming to arrange this. The house, they said, was worth nothing. I left a message that if the heirs would leave the cottage and its contents and give me access I might want to buy some of the contents. I came back to find that the cottage was empty and the contents burnt or thrown into the stream. Much the same thing happened at Evanton in Easter Ross. I hope to tell how I averted such a tragedy, managed to save at least one doomed article, at Kyle of Lochalsh.

I have never been able to trace the origin of this unwillingness to sell the belongings of the dead. I do not think that it was fear of infection for the Highlanders seem to be quite unaware of the risks, often disastrously in the case of tuberculosis.

As my collection grew it took more and more time to look up and arrange. My efforts at repairs and conservation were very simple. The untreated wool used in home-spun blankets is more palatable to moths than more sophisticated fabrics. I should imagine some of the modern 'man-made' ones would give the poor things indigestion. I found that liberal sprinklings of camphor crystals between the folds of the blankets were quite effective.

In the case of the implements, I tried to rub off the rust with sandpaper and to give a rub with an oily cloth to keep them free of it. Wood beetles were a worse menace. All too many things one longed to possess had been ruined by their excavations. Comparatively few of the things that I did acquire were free of them and one knew that the newly hatched beetles that emerged from them would lay their own eggs within other exhibits. They are called 'death watch' beetles because they make a ticking noise by hitting their heads on the wood as their mating call. I used to prowl around the collection at night trying to spot such calls. I must have been responsible for the death of thousands of wood beetles. The method that I used was to paint the affected surface with Cuprinol.

7

Collecting in the Islands

O LD age plays funny tricks with one's memories. I remember the happy carefree collecting in familiar country that I did before the Inverness Exhibition very clearly. But the later trips to the western Highlands and Islands that I made after I had started the Folk Museum are jumbled together in my mind and I have forgotten many names of places and of people. I had gained a general idea where it would be most rewarding to go from trips that I had taken when writing *In the Tracks of Montrose* and *The Lordship of the Isles*.

Wherever the museum was – at Iona, Laggan or Kingussie – I took the chance when travelling to or from the Western Isles of planning my route so as to pass likely places. From Edinburgh to Oban one could go by the south side of Loch Tay and visit the interesting little settlement of Ardeonaig and make a detour to Ballachulish. While I still had the museum I was writing a history of the MacLeods and had the great pleasure of staying at Dunvegan and working on the family muniments and I could cross to Skye by the Kyle Rhea ferry (the old crossing place for the cattle in the droving days) by taking the road up Glen Garry and Glen Shiel. This beautiful area, so often mentioned in Highland history, was not rewarding from the collecting point of view. My memories are of being stuck behind a slow and obstinate caravan almost as far as Tomdoun, of surprising a stag who was dozing and sunning himself on the warm road and seeing him off and away over the steep rough hill track with extraordinary grace and speed. As I watched I well understood the special position red deer have in Highland tradition. Poets sang of the grace and beauty of stag and hind but also of the prowess of the lone hunter who also figures in tales of witches and the sidhe. Great organised deer drives figured in the most distinguished form of Highland entertainment. Oisean (transformed into Ossian by Macpherson), the chronicler of the Feinne, was the child of Finn and of a hind and when his mother began to lick him as a mother does naturally with her calf, hair grew where her tongue had touched him and he had a patch of hair above one eyebrow. I treasure this tale because it was actually told me by a countryman on Lismore, one of the very few that one was actually told. But the real joy was driving through the larch-wood plantings covering the slopes beyond Loch Duich. Through the trees, changing in their beauty at all times of the year, one caught sudden glimpses of far off seas and lochs. The alternate routes to Oban were more rewarding.

My visits to the Outer Hebrides were limited to the more accessible of the islands. They were fascinating in their great diversity. I was always conscious of the lack of trees. When I got back to the mainland I always felt that I could go and hug the trunk of the first well-grown one that I came to but when I commented upon this to an exiled Islander she replied, 'Trees! Nasty, untidy things!' The clean planes of the machair and the long stretches of shore and sand have a special beauty. Once, when staying at Lochboisdale a little before the date of the local games, I had crossed to the west coast (which was always easy to do for a kindly passing motorist would invariably give one a lift in the old spirit of Highland hospitality and would get the true reward of a country man in finding out who the stranger was and what had brought him or her to the locality) and I was delighted to hear the sound of pipes and to find in sheltered hollows in the dunes about half a dozen local pipers busily practising for the great event. It is good to know that in South Uist the old tradition of local piping had been kept up and I learn that it still continues to be so.

I have a special memory of a bicycle ride from Grimersta Lodge in what the member of the staff who lent me the bike called 'a brisk brattle of wind' and which I thought was a howling gale. Throughout the ride I did not pedal once. Going – I had to push the bike in the teeth of the gale and coming back – I freewheeled, carried along by the wind. The manageress of the Highland Home Industries Association in Edinburgh had kindly given me two addresses. The two houses were near each other and also to Dun Carloway, one of the finest brochs in the Hebrides. Of course, I took a break from my collecting to take a good look at it. I noticed the hollow walls though I did not climb up to the top. It belongs to the time when Scotland had almost emerged into history.

I first visited a modern house built upon a slight rise to give a good view. It was well built but that day it felt like a sail in the wind which boomed in the chimneys, rattled everything that was loose and, where one window had been left a chink open, raised the carpet in billows. Even when everything was shut, one could still feel its pressure.

The other house was built in the traditional style of the Long Island and some of the Northern Isles – the low dry-stone walls were double – about three feet apart and the space between filled with sand or gravel. The ends were rounded. The roof – also low – was formed of a framework of light timbers, covered with layers of sods and of thatch and it rested upon the inside wall, so that there was a wide ledge all round the house, for all the rainwater drained through the core of sand and the house remained stone dry. It was a style perfectly suited to a wet, very stormy land and was built of local materials with the minimum of wood. Of course, I had seen a number of houses of this type and noticed local differences in these of Lewis and other islands but it was a new experience to be inside one in such a gale. As one entered, there was a feeling of relief and calm. The wind passed over the house without a sound or disturbance. The dry-stone roof of sods and thatch kept out the cold in winter far more effectively than did the well-built, stone Georgian house of the museum itself.

A characteristic feature of the Long Island has disappeared with the making of carriageways across the North and the South Fords. The North Ford is between North Uist and Benbecula via Grimsay, and the South Ford is between Benbecula and South Uist. Almost always, I reached these islands upon different expeditions and I only actually crossed the North Ford on a trip from Benbecula. That was upon a perfect day. The tide was in and we crossed by boat. The golden sand below the shallow water was freckled with the dancing reflections of the sunlit ripples above. The tangle which one usually only sees when the tide is out, lying in a tangled mass along the shore, was erect and swaying gracefully in the slight movement of the water, its deeper richer colour contrasting with the radiance of the sunlit sand. This, of course, was a most favourable crossing. One heard many tales of races to get across before the Ford closed and of the incoming tide coming up to the axles of the wheels as the horses were urged to a gallop to reach the shore in time. Of course, there were also tales of fatalities.

I was more familiar with the South Ford. I spent some days at Creagorry on the Benbecula side of the Ford. The hotel was one of the most friendly that I ever stayed in. I got a kindly lift and managed to get to Bernera to do some collecting. I was even more successful when I crossed the Ford to South Uist. The whole atmosphere there was pleasant and congenial. There was an excellent relationship between the local priest and the local minister and among the country people themselves. I obtained a great many of the very things that I was anxious to get including a séisach – a long wooden seat, a piece of furniture that was very characteristic of the homely comfortable setting of the main living room of the house after a hearth on the ground in the middle of the house had been replaced by a fire at one end of the room against a partition wall and a fireplace with a wide wooden hood. One pictures the ceilidhs that continued to be held with a continuance of the songs and tales traditional and of the dry wit often expressed in verse, for a characteristic of the people's art was their talent for improvisation. In one's mind's eye one pictures a row of people taking their full part in the entertainment, and not a mere audience as is the modern imitation of a ceilidh, sitting on one of the old séisachs.

I crossed very often when the Ford was open. At all times it was fascinating to watch especially when it was due to close. I was staying at Creagorry in calm weather. The tide only came in very slowly and as a slow ripple. But in front of it, the sand became wet and the puddles and shallow pools began to spread and to deepen. The exact time of its closing varied a little according to how much wind was blowing. One day when I crossed, my watch was wrong and I had miscalculated. When I was about the middle, the sand became wetter and wetter and I had to wade through what had been little more than a puddle. The going became heavier and heavier. I was not in any danger but, as I neared the shore, men who had been working in a field and had seen me, arrived running. I was quickly taken to a nearby cottage, a large dram was more or less poured into me, and I was set down beside a roaring fire. There I stayed, surrounded by warmth and friendliness until the water was deep enough for a boat to be launched to take me back to Benbecula. The Ford, however, could be extremely dangerous. There was a channel in the northern side of it where, I was told, not long before a waggonette full of people had become stuck. It had been a risky business to get the passengers safely through rough deepening water to land. The lad who had taken a leading part in doing so was pointed out to me. He was pale and slight and not at all of the athletic type.

The glory of the northern Hebrides is the transfiguration of the colourings that fitfully visits them. Among my random memories of those collecting trips is of the first half-hour of a visit to Eriskay. As I scrambled up the exceedingly slippery landing place, the sky, the long low stretch of land, the sand and the glassy sea were all of a uniform but slightly lighter or darker grey. Then, in a matter of minutes, everything began, by imperceptible degrees, to change. The land became patterned in green and brown. The sand at first gleamed palely and then became a white that was incandescent in its intensity. It actually radiated light. The sky, faintly blue, seemed remote compared to the intensity of the colours of the earth. The green of the sea in the shallows, like the white of the sand, was luminous in its purity. Further out, the dazzle of the ripples blurred the darkness of the rocks as one looked at them.

One has heard accounts so often and indeed expects such exhibitions of brilliant colouring in the rather stark setting of the northern Hebrides. I was privileged to see a totally unexpected vision of colouring in Islay. In contrast to the northern Islands, Islay has fertile fields, fine stock, trees, and shapely green hills. It was, therefore, a place where one felt happy to be but it had not the outstanding scenery of for instance, parts of Skye, yet, upon a day of days, when I happened to be going along the shores of Loch Gruinart, the colouring of the loch was transformed. The shallows became a pale pure green, the deeper channels which threaded their way out of them an intense blue and as the loch widened, reaches of dancing, dazzling ripples spread across it and then were merged into the great shining plain of the calm sea. About Islay moreover more than about any of the Islands for me at least there always seems to cling a remembrance of the past and of the times when it was the centre of 'The Lordship of the Isles'.

Another sight that I shall not easily forget is that from the northern tip of Lewis. Great green waves holding their unbroken spray from the polar region beyond the horizon, with crests of gleaming foam and hearts of intense, shining emerald green were smashing themselves upon the Snout of the Butt of Lewis, the surface of the wet black rock shining in the pale northern sunlight.

The Long Island has many historical associations. One's

mind is carried back to Prince Charles Edward and far beyond to the tragic end of the MacLeods of Lewis and yet further back to the raiding Norsemen, but for me the memory that most recalls the past is that of the stone circle at Callanish, especially when I saw the great groups of monoliths at dusk on my way back to Grimersta where I was staying for a few days. When one thinks that during the best part of 2,000 years – about as long as the period during which Scotland has actually been recorded in history – men with only the help of stone tools could possibly set up, extend and alter that assembly of great stones – of the devotion that inspired their labours and the constancy that made them continue the work – of the organisation that enabled the large number of men that must have been required when the only means of effort was literally manpower – one is lost in admiration for stone-age man.

Of this stock of lasting impressions that particular places have left in my mind, the one that I treasured most is waiting beside the ruins of the chapel on Colonsay for the tide to ebb and the ford to Oronsay to open. The way across is marked by stones set upright in the sand. There is a burial ground with a beautiful standing cross at Oronsay and one could imagine how the mourners waited, as I was waiting, by the chapel and the petitions that they must have raised for the soul of the dead that they were carrying to Oronsay. A feeling of the sanctity of the place came over me. I recalled the beautiful island legends of how Our Lady and the Child would meet and mingle with simple people. I knew that the coming of a realisation of such Presences was not limited to lovely, lonely places – indeed far the reverse for those who have true spirituality. But the weakest souls, such as my own, can only feel thankful when to be in such a place bestows that feeling of all enfolding Blessedness.

8

Ardnamurchan, Arisaig and Kyle of Lochalsh

I CANNOT remember on which of my expeditions I made a foray into Ardnamurchan from Acharacle. It was not a success. I did not get anything. I was most anxious to see the arrangements in the house that Miss M E M Donaldson had built in the traditional style but with modifications to suit modern ways of living, including 'mod cons'. I have always thought this was a splendid idea. The style of these houses not only made the best use of the materials that were locally available but was especially suitable for local weather conditions. It had been evolved during successive generations of a highly intelligent people. When I had seen the sections of half-ready-made houses, more suitable for the Home Counties of England than the Hebrides, being imported wholesale, I had deplored the lack of vision by the authorities responsible. I thought that Miss Donaldson was pioneering a most valuable idea and I very much wanted to see what her house was like. I had, however, looked forward to calling upon her with some trepidation for she could be a formidable lady and I knew that in some respects we did not see eye to eye. It was not with unmixed disappointment that I learned that she was from home. I went to have a look at the outside of the house. This was hampered by the presence of a very inquisitive bull. Unfortunately the house is there no more – it was accidentally burnt down.

Another trip to a point upon the west coast was along the Mallaig road to Lochailort in Arisaig. I got a warm welcome from the owner of the hotel, Miss Williamina Macrae. She had felt the pull of her Highland roots and had returned to live and face the hard facts of making a living in a country of her treasured traditions and romances. F Marion McNeill, best known for her work upon Scots cooking and Highland traditional cures, was a fellow guest. It was pleasant to swap experiences with her. I got some information. She gave the museum a nice write-up in an article she was writing. While wandering about, I came upon a group of abandoned cottages. The thatch and sods of the roofs had gone but the wooden framework was almost intact. It is a district of small trees and scrub. The light timbers of which the roofs were made were most skilfully planned so as not to put them under too great a strain from the heavy peat covering of the roofs and they were very neatly fastened together with wooden pegs. This was an early trip when the museum was still in Iona and it was bitterly frustrating that there was no place there where one of them could be re-erected. In any case there were no funds for transporting and re-erecting it. While I was at Lochailort I was constantly told of the finds that I was likely to make upon the coastline beyond Lochailort and in the hills behind it. The problem was how to get there and take away anything I could acquire. There was only a track, unsuitable for wheeled vehicles, and it was too far for me to walk to. The thought of this El Dorado for a folk museum collector remained at the back of my mind and when I got to Kingussie a possible solution appeared. Jimmockie Mackintosh hired excellent ponies for carrying shot stags in forests or for conveying tourists upon pony treks. I thought I would hire a pony and spring cart and also a pack saddle and panniers, that I could drive as far as I could, then put the panniers on the pony and if I got weary myself ride on top of them. The plan had got as far as a friendly correspondence with Mr Cameron Head of Inverailort just when I was able to hand over the Folk Museum to the Scottish universities. Shortly afterwards, a road was made along that bit of coast and probably a good many of the vestiges of the old way of life have been lost.

The country around the Kyle of Lochalsh was specially rewarding. I had made an earlier stay there and among other places visited the little settlement at Drumbuie, and after I had moved the Folk Museum to Kingussie Mrs MacDougall of MacDougall said she would go with me on another trip. While it was under discussion, one of her daughters managed to go on a drive with me. It was to a tailor who was extremely good at making tartan skirts – which at that time were much worn and to my mind are vastly preferable to 'jeans'. She admitted after-wards that she had planned it to satisfy herself that I was really fit to drive her mother upon the difficult roads we would have to drive upon during our trip. Fortunately I passed this test.

Our first port of call was Balmacara. From there it was easy to visit Loch Duich. Kintail is a particularly interesting district. It is the only place on the mainland where I saw a man using a cas chrom. He was working apparently without difficulty on a slope so steep that I think a plough team would scarcely have managed. He was making a very straight furrow. Although slypes had long gone out of use and I failed to secure a specimen, the people remembered using them on these slopes. They con-sisted of a primitive kind of sledge made of two shafts with a few boards nailed between them. Loch Duich is also a place of magical beauty. The group of hills above it – the Five Sisters of Kintail – seem to me to have the virginal charm of extreme youth in the purity of their gracious lines. In contrast to the bare vertical lines of the peaks is the infinite complexity of the coast-line with its abundant vegetation and tangle-covered rocks and in front of that the wide flat surface of the sea-loch that mirrors all the complex loveliness above and then breaks it up by shining lines of ripples.

On our way north we stopped for tea at Eilean Donan Castle. Set on its little island in Loch Duich where that loch meets Loch Alsh and Loch Long and with a splendid background of great slopes rising to the hills, its looks do not belie its stormy past, when the Macraes stoutly held it in trust for their great and friendly neighbours, the Mackenzies. It was most interesting to see inside it. It had been conscientiously restored. The only apparent innovation is the bridge. But upon a dull afternoon very little light penetrated through small windows set in enormously thick walls and I felt confirmed in my heretical belief that ancient castles are best kept as well preserved ruins or only restored for use upon ceremonial occasions. Of course, when they have been continuously lived in and a descendant has restored the old fabric in accordance with its own period, as is the case at Dunvegan Castle, the greater comfort can be enjoyed with a clear conscience.

It was sad to see how much the condition of Drumbuie had deteriorated since my last visit but we had great success there. As I have already pointed out, the most important thing in collecting in the Highlands is to have a 'connecting link' – a mutual acquaintance. High and low, Mrs MacDougall had them in abundance. Two acquisitions stand out in my memory. One of them is of a chimney. During my journeys, I had learnt to distinguish three outstandingly different local types of old houses with some lesser variants but in their earliest forms they all had a hearth on the floor in the middle of the house and the smoke had, in all of them, to find its own way through an aperture in the roof. In the course of my travels I have only been inside two houses with such a primitive kind of fireplace but I saw plenty of the ruins of cottages in different districts that showed traces of this arrangement. In all the old styles the construction of a chimney with a flue at the gable end was not included. There are any amount of later ruins of cottages with such a feature but this style was only introduced with the great agricultural reforms and it is not indigenous. The old local styles of cottages in the north west and in the Hebrides had rounded ends. Those in the south western Highlands had gable ends. In the eastern and central Highlands the most ancient ones that I saw when I did my past collecting for the Inverness Exhibition, depended upon the couples and not the walls for their main support and had square ends with hipped ends to their roofs. In almost all these local styles the earliest chimneys were made of wood and were built against a central partition. The fireplace had stone hobs and the chimney was made with a wooden hood over the fire to draw in all the smoke, with a long tube of wood narrowing to a chimney above the roof. They were known as 'hanging chimneys' – *similear crochaidh*.

I was much interested in the remains of these chimneys and pointed them out to Mrs MacDougall and while we were looking round a group of older buildings beside a modern croft she called out to me, 'Do you want to buy a chimney?' She was standing near one within the shell of a ruined building. I replied, 'Yes, if I can get it intact to Kingussie!' She turned to the crofter to whom she had been chatting and asked, 'What about that?' and he replied, 'Easy enough!' I bought it for less than the freight to Kingussie. As the chimney had been built quite separately from the partition wall and narrowed from end to end, it was sawn into three sections which slipped into one another, were securely done up with rope like a big parcel and arrived safely at Kingussie.

In some districts, especially in Mull, more modern fireplaces or stoves were sometimes built at the rounded end of a cottage and the jauntiest looking little chimney was incorporated with the end of the roof-tree and the thatch was brought up its sides. I always wished that I could have obtained and rebuilt one of them.

The second achievement of this trip was the removal of a kist from a deserted house. I came across this tradition three times and the deliberate destruction of the contents of two others. I think that it was partly due to the very prevalent idea that it was derogatory to one's dignity to own the old-fashioned 'troke'. In the case discussed earlier of the burning of the contents of a cottage, I am sure that this was in order to forestall an attempt by me to get them for the museum. But I am certain there exists some deeper feeling that goes very much further back.

In any case, in the course of our wanderings, we found an empty cottage, rather dilapidated but fully furnished. We learnt that its owner had died and that her nearest relative, I think a niece, lived close by. We went to see her. We pointed out that the things in the cottage were lying there unused and asked her if she wished to dispose of them. She said that she did not want to sell any of them. In the course of the conversation she said that the cottage was not worth repairing and that the roof would soon fall in. This happens very often to old cottages when the thatch is not kept in very good repair. The heavy roof of peat becomes sodden and so heavy as to break the wooden framework that supports it. I had seen through the window a wooden kist with a very interesting ornamentation. The survival of styles in furniture has been of special interest to me and I was very disappointed when she again refused to sell it. She saw this. She smiled and said that she would not sell it but that she would give it to me. We hurried in to get it. Fortunately it was empty and so we could carry it straight out. Nevertheless while we were doing so I thought to myself if we were breaking some ancient taboo the decrepit roof might choose that moment to fall about our ears. We escaped that nemesis.

9

Applecross and the Sea

I DID not work my way north visiting the most likely areas conscientiously but I made a point of visiting Applecross very early in my collecting trips because I hoped that from there I could visit a farm that I was told was still being cultivated by joint-farmers in scattered holdings. Making my way northwards from Kyle of Lochalsh to Loch Carron, I was glad to notice that the tide was in. The jetty at the ferry across the Loch was still very primitive and when the tide was out, to drive onto the ferry-boat was rather an ordeal. Later on I was deeply to regret that, as I drove back along and had noticed a wickerwork door on a shed by the roadside, I had not stopped and tried to acquire it. I thought that it would be a nuisance to take it along and that therefore it would be better to try to get it on the way back – also, at the back of my mind was the thought of the jetty. I hurried on and when, upon my return journey, I stopped to enquire about it, the door had just been destroyed. I was to realise that wickerwork has a very low rate of survival and that it was an important Highland craft. I was to seek over and over again for a wickerwork door and never again come near to getting one.

The old road to Applecross took the same way over the hills as had the older drove-road. It went by the Bealach nam Bo – the Pass of the Cattle. The slope up to the pass is very steep and the road took a very direct line up it with several hairpin bends. My engine became over-heated and so, on reaching the top, although I knew I was being wicked, I cut off the engine and let the car trickle down the gentle slope at the top of the pass. The car moved soundlessly and it surprised an eagle upon the ground close to the road. I was much struck by the length of his legs – of course, eagles when flying, tuck them close to their bodies. Rather clumsily he scrambled on to a low rock from which to take off and then to soar upwards in magnificent flight.

I did a little collecting in Applecross. I got a chair that showed the influence of a Victorian style. Saint Maelrubha, the Irish evangelist who brought Christianity to the northern Highlands, is buried at Applecross. In the old days, it was regarded as a sanctuary and public opinion was deeply shocked when once it was raided. It was deeply distressing to observe the intense bitterness that existed when I was there between the members of the Established and Free Churches. A minister of the former had come to hold a service. The owner of the guesthouse where I was staying was a strong upholder of the latter. When it came to going to church on Sunday, I felt rather like the baby in Solomon's judgement as I was pressed into accompanying the members of the rival denominations to their place of worship and I wondered what the old saintly evangelist, Saint Maelrubha, would think of his disciples.

While staying at Applecross I walked over to Kishorn, then a very quiet little scatter of houses. A woman met me at one door. She had money in her hand and asked me if I was collecting for something. She was evidently prepared to give me something. After explaining what I was after, I asked her if she would have given me money whatever it was that I was collecting for. She replied that she would not like to send a stranger from the door empty-handed. Such was the true spirit of Highland hospitality.

The farm that I was anxious to see was about eight miles up the coast and only a track led to it. I thought that I might hire a garron and ride there but I was warned that there were several gates that I might not be able to open so I gave myself a treat and hired the lobster fisherman's boat – a dinghy with an out-board motor engine. The remembrance of the trip there and back stimulates other recollections. The farm itself, when I got to it, was a landward community. The people there took the opportunity of buying some fish from the boatman. They evidently never thought of taking a boat onto the sea loch and catching fish for themselves. I am sure that they thought I was an emissary of some kind sent to pry and they were guarded when I approached them. The houses were not traditional nor were the plenishings of the one into which I was invited. I do not know the acreage of the farm or of the individual shares of the joint-tenants of which there were less than half a dozen. They were obviously following a rotation of crops, and such implements as I saw were not archaic. The outstanding visible difference was that they had their share of land in scattered portions – I think ten portions in the case of the man whom I found to be most approachable.

There was no sign of the serious overcrowding and distressing poverty that had existed in the settlements of the kelp-burners after the collapse of that industry nor of the very low standard of living of the old joint-tenants in the days before the Agricultural Revolution. In those days rigs allotted to a joint-tenant were not in a block but dispersed over the in-field. The reason always given in writings upon the subject for such an inconvenient arrangement was that it ensured an equal effort to cultivate the whole ground by the group of workers. I always wondered if there was not also another one and I was much intrigued to know why the system had persisted upon this farm where one team of animals did not any longer draw a wooden plough or bands of reapers gather the harvest. It was to ensure some equality in the returns to each joint tenant from land that was undrained and was very uneven in the quality of the crops that it bore. The farm was upon fairly flat but undulating ground and looking at the little patches one did notice a variation when one compared one patch of crop – notably turnip – with another.

I did not reap as much benefit as I had hoped from visiting the farm but the trip in the boat was a great treat. I had given myself a similar one when I was writing *The Lordship of the Isles*. I had been able to make an excuse for allowing myself a longer trip by boat from Colonsay to Islay. Travelling by small boat instead of by steamer makes a surprisingly great difference to what one sees of the land- and sea-scapes. The scale of proportions is altered so that there is an actual alteration in what one sees. But there is also an added faculty for sensing the reality of the past – that it actually happened to people like oneself upon tangible earth and water and that its effects are like strands of varying thicknesses woven into the fabric of our present-day life.

I am a landlubber. All my Highland connections are with the eastern and central Highlands. The only fisher community with which I had contact was upon the east coast when my parents rented, for some years, a house on the Kincardinshire coast. In those days there were still communities of line-fishermen close to where we lived, with whom my father made friendly contact. They were full-time fishermen who kept themselves very much apart from the landward folk. They had their own traditions and way of life, and it is ten thousand pities that no effort was made to make a serious study or comprehensive record of them. But of course, even if one is only a fairly well-read tripper, one has a general idea of things in the past. My trip by boat to and from the farm was especially rewarding in enabling my mind to visualise something of the remote past that has helped to shape the present everyday people of the western Highlands and Islands. The surface of the changeful sea is timeless and the outlines of its shores are constant. One gets a far deeper sense of this from a small boat than from a steamer and I treasure the memory of those two sea-borne trips because one felt that one was seeing the land actually from the same angle as did the seafarers from times before history.

I knew that the ancient Gael (like the modern Arran Islanders, at least in a famous film, and most surprisingly, up to the eighteenth century, the people of Strathspey) used boats made of hides stretch upon a wooden frame. I loved the legend of Saint

83

Brendan – that when he set out to find the Earthly Paradise he failed, until Saint Ita told him that he would never reach it in a boat made of death-stained hides. He then set out in a boat made of wood and eventually reached the land of his heart's desire. And of course it is common knowledge that Saint Columba landed on Iona from a curragh, for the name of the bay where he did so records the fact. It was in coracles too, that he old Gaelic saints, Maelrubha, Kenneth and the others, brought to the little settlements of people all along the western coast the Christian faith.

The Norse galleys which later came to harry those Western Isles and coastlands were beautiful though terrible. Of lovely lines, they were painted, bedecked with shields and full of magnificent fighting men. I have read several Norse Sagas in translation and upon a later visit to Norway was to see the Gokstad ship – imbued, even in a landlubber's eyes, with speed and power. The Sagas have many passages in praise of their galleys. The terse prose matched the vigour, the enterprise of the race that penetrated the ancient strongholds of Europe and into regions far beyond, but the ruthless lack of morality of the Saga, 'Burnt Njal', produced in me the same revulsion as one feels for the decadent horror stories of today. Much later I began to realise that having access to iron ore had naturally encouraged the Norse to be workers in iron, which had enabled them to build their extremely efficient ships. This is as well as their extraordinary energy and reckless courage had enabled them to use their galleys as they had. On Iona I had seen the spot where the monks had been massacred and I knew that the Gaels had had to abandon that isle of their holiest associations to the heathen raiders. One could feel glad that one lived in an age when the peaceful waters of the sea lochs were not infested with such dreadful shipping. The Vikings, however, stayed to settle – the very high proportion of Norse place names in Lewis and to a lesser extent in other parts of the western Highlands and Islands proves this – and one wonders whether, in the more quiescent periods that followed, the possession of iron and the skill to use it gave their agriculture a superiority over that of the earlier settlers. A mixed race arose, but it was Gaelic, the language of the invaded, that they spoke and it was from Erin that they took their culture and it was Gaelic my boatmen spoke together though one of them was blond and ruddy as any Viking.

I think of Somerled as the outstanding figure in the situation that developed in this mixed race. By name he was Norse, but he had a pedigree that traced his descent from Conn of the Hundred Battles, High King of Erin, and to a yet more distant mythical ancestry. By inheritance and conquest he gained mastery of nearly all of the Western Isles and a large part of the western mainland. He sired the founders of the two oldest clans in Scotland – the MacDougalls and the MacDonalds. He met his end in 1164 when he was leading an expedition of 160 galleys, probably in resistance to the encroaching power of the Scots-Norman family of the Stewarts.

Until the thirteenth century there were competing claims by the kings of Scotland and Norway for the overlordship of the Western Isles. I picture King Haakon's great attempt to make good his claim. He gathered further support in the Orkneys and sailed on with 100 galleys. As he made his way down the Western Isles, their rulers were faced with an agonising clash of loyalties and the lands of those who remained loyal to the King of Scots were plundered. Rothesay Castle was attacked but resisted all attempts to break its defences and finally, off Arran, a violent storm worked havoc with the fleet and the Norsemen were defeated at Largs when they attempted to land. Haakon and the poor remnant of his fleet sailed back to Orkney where he died. In 1266 the sovereignty of the Western Isles was surrendered to the King of Scots. Of Somerled's descendants, one branch that descended from his grandson Donald attained a predominant position and assumed the title of Lord of the Isles. It is only fitting that a lymphad, a heraldic anglification of the Gaelic for 'long ship', should be emblazoned upon the armorial bearings of the Lords of the Isles and their successors. In the poetry and stories of the times, galleys are much in evidence. They were woven into the administrative and social system of the times and the service of a galley with a specified number of oars became a regular due from the land-holders of the Islands and the coasts. For instance, in the seventeenth century, MacLeod of MacLeod had to supply the services of three galleys and a birlinn, a smaller boat of the same kind, as dues for his lands. Very often their likenesses were carved upon the grave-slabs of the period. No doubt this was as a status symbol and they must also have represented a most deeply prized possession of the man whom the stone commemorated. Quite obviously, although to fit them into the shape of the grave-slab they are not represented as having the high sharply raked stern of the Gokstad Ship, there is however a good deal of evidence that they did have it. Otherwise the resemblance is very close to the ancient Viking galley. Because of later developments it is worthwhile considering them further although I can only use the language of a landlubber in trying to describe them. They were largely boats for rowing, not sailing. The sail, what a sailor would call a 'lug-sail', was set at right angles to the boat and was only of use when a favourable wind blew the boat along. Otherwise a large number of oarsmen had to row it. We know that a galley had 26 oars and a birlinn 16 oars. Of course, like the complement of a ship of HMS, the crew was intended for fighting as well as navigation. The galley itself had no keel. It skimmed on the top of the water. To claim that Kintyre was an island, the King of Norway had himself carried in a galley across the isthmus of Tarbert in Kintyre. The word 'tarbert' signified a place where boats could be carried across a narrow piece of land to avoid a long and dangerous voyage round projecting land. Tarbert was a common place-name. I can think of three straight away.

Galleys continued in use for centuries. They are mentioned in the bitter struggles attending the acquisition of dominance by the Mackenzies. In the last serious attempt to re-establish the

Lordship of the Isles, by Donald Dhu in 1545, no less than 180 galleys were assembled by his supporters. Their leader, one of the most luckless figures in history, fell ill and died. The fleet, like that of his ancestor Somerled, dispersed. During the sixteenth century, galleys were still used by the great maritime powers as well as technically superior sailing craft but later than that their use diminished even in the Highlands. One of the demands that James VI and the Scots Privy Council made upon a group of the west Highland chiefs was that they should supply a list of their galleys. Nine chiefs, including the great Argyll, had only six galleys and six birlinns, but they also had a number of boats. As a further demand in his extraordinarily harsh and insulting treatment of his west Highland subjects, James then ordered the chiefs of that area to give up having boats at all and they replied that their livelihood and the cattle trade (so convenient for England) would be impossible without them. It is significant that the last entry in the MacLeod of MacLeod accounts relating to galleys or birlinns was made in 1706, for 30 yards of plaiding to make a sail for MacLeod's birlinn at a cost of 24 merks. Later entries refer to the occasional hire of boats.

As far as the traditional histories of the clans are concerned, those of the west Highlands and Islands relating to earlier centuries abound with tales of raids and of visits from island to island for festivities. The waterways that are now deserted were once busy with boats coming and going as an integral part of the people's daily life, and also of their troubled fate. When the great Lordship of the Isles was in its last turbulent years, under pressure from outside, divided and misgoverned within, there was a great sea-fight between its warring factions in the Bay of Tobermory and a clan history tells of how the galleys of the leading opponents grappled together and of how the victors boarded the galley of the vanquished. Among all the many tales about boats, one story happens to stick in my mind because on a long walk that I took in Lewis, I visited the crumbling earthworks of the old stronghold of Dun Eistean perched above the shores of the Minch. It was once one of the homes of the Morrisons and in the constantly renewed quarrels between this lesser clan and the MacLeods of Lewis, the MacLeods in some force made surprise attacks upon it. To shorten a dramatic story, Allan Mór Morrison, the leader, and his two brothers, finally had to make their escape by boat. They were pursued by larger parties in two boats and Allan Mór was so strong that in the desperate flight he pulled an oar on one side of the boat while his brothers pulled the two oars on the other side. To encourage them he composed and sang an iorram (rowing song) as they rowed and this became a popular song among the people of Lewis. Finally, Allan Mór's boat was overtaken and after prodigious acts of valour he and his brothers were killed.

All that I have written so far is, no doubt, well known already to most people but now there arise three rather obvious problems that so far as I know have not been seriously tackled. The gradual abandonment of the use of the galley by the leading men of the Isles and western Highlands raises an unanswered question in my mind. We know that the people of Inverness conducted an important trade, carrying meal and other goods in exchange for herrings and salmon and other products. The account book of worthy Bailie Steuart and the voluminous Culloden Papers abound with interesting details. We know that younger sons of the gentry in the eastern Highlands became merchants and took part in this trade. Why did not those of the west coast use their galleys or equally large boats and themselves carry on and develop this local trading or indeed launch further afield? At a later stage in the eighteenth century the younger son of MacLeod of Bernera owned a ship engaged in the East India trade and made a fortune. It is strange that more members of a race with such a long and fine tradition of seamanship should not have found an outlet from the overcrowding home in this way.

When, secondly, did the west Highlanders abandon the lugsail, which was useless in a contrary wind, in favour of a sail that would enable the sailors to tack and by oblique moves force an adverse wind to bring them to their destination? Accounts lead one to think that, highly intelligent and not given to over-working as they are, the Highlanders were remarkably slow in doing so. Rowing songs survive and even eighteenth century writers such as Boswell record how the boatmen sang as they rowed. That magnificent sea poem, 'Clan Ranald's Galley', was written by Alexander Macdonald (Alasdair MacMhaigihstir) who died about 1770. Nostalgia alone cannot have inspired his vivid detailed account of the voyage to Erin. The shape of the ships by the eighteenth century, according to John Knox, was extremely bad. From casual references, one gathered that in many districts the sterns were straight and no longer raked, although the Orkney fishermen stuck to this characteristic and it is probably from them that the Moray Firth fishermen derived their 'scaffies' – fishing boats of outstanding performance with raked sterns and curved stems.

I very much regret that as a landlubber and only conversant with freshwater fishing, I did not make more effort to collect the relics of the old Highland fisheries. (I may say in palliation that traditions and gear of the line fishermen of Kincardinshire and Aberdeenshire with their exceptionally important historical and theological associations have in my own day been wantonly allowed to disappear unstudied, unrewarded, ignored). The government record with regard to the west coast fishermen is a bad one. In medieval times, the Royal Burghs were granted exclusive rights over the herring fisheries and after this became obsolete, the Dutch fishermen, with better boats, were allowed to monopolise it and in addition the home fishermen were hampered by a crippling Salt-Tax. With the Continental Wars of the eighteenth century, government policy changed. The Salt-Tax was repealed, the Dutch fishing boats were driven off, bounties were offered and, at a later stage, harbours and piers were built. In 1786 people of position founded the British Fisheries Society. A lasting memorial to their efforts is the lay-out of Tobermory, designed to be a local centre for the industry. Frankly, I do not know all the ins and outs of the failure of the industry. It is a story in which the perverse habits of migrating herring shoals play some part and human misunderstanding a good deal more. The derelict harbour at Leverburgh in Harris is the most woeful reminder of defeated hopes and enterprise. Nevertheless some living traditions have been preserved and the fisheries are not dead.

I was lucky enough to learn something of the folk-lore of the fishermen of Barra by word of mouth as well as from Carmichael's book. I have had the pleasure of actually hearing from Mr Donald Macdonald the thrilling account of the landings of the fishing boats upon the open shores of Lewis when the Atlantic rollers were sweeping up to that bare, sandy shore and I am certain that in each case a long tradition lies behind such stories and such skill. But a great gap of ignorance has been allowed to develop between the near and the distant past. I was landward-minded, not only because of my own circumstances but because of the main content of any available reading material, and I did not think about such problems until I tried to tackle the subject in *Highland Folk Ways* long after my collecting days were over. I am sorry that I did not find out more. I am much more so that no one else tackled the job long before. Local fishing has indeed declined but the old seafaring instinct survives in the large proportion of Islanders who fare further afield and serve in the Royal Navy and the Merchant Service.

There is a third problem that I cannot solve. Why do the local people never seem to enjoy their wonderful facilities for boating? They play shinty, they compete in local Highland games. They never seem to go sailing for their own pleasure or indulge in boat races or water sports. The townies of Edinburgh by contrast flock to the Forth to enjoy a sail or they convey their little yachts to more extensive waters. Why has sailing not had the same attraction to the Highlanders?

I chugged along, a passenger in a boat that I had hired to

take me to and from the farm. I recalled highly romantic episodes of the remote past and I watched the gannets plunging above the sea and the buzzards wheeling over the cliffs but, at that stage, I had not begun to puzzle my head over the problems of the fishing industry. Later on, in making the museum, I never attempted to give it the important place that it deserved. I was ignorant of this aspect of Highland life when I started the museum. I learnt a bit. In trying to do so I discovered that compared to acres of written matter about the landward life of the crofters, made of every variety of approach from the aridly academic to the lushly folksy, very little has been written about the history of the fisheries and the changes in the boats and methods of navigation – but I would not, of course, have been able to illustrate them at *Am Fasgadh*, had I tried.

10

The North-West
and Highland Buildings

UP the north-west coast from Inverewe to Laide was a very good hunting ground for me. The things that I was searching for were there. I met with great friendliness and hospitality and made valuable contacts. I stayed at Inverewe with the Sawyers in the days before it was gifted to the National Trust. I was there before the flowering of the rhododendrons, so beloved of Osgood Mackenzie, and their foliage beneath the pine trees looked very sombre. But there was a fine old-fashioned Scots kitchen garden. Of course, the flowering season in the grounds has now been much prolonged. Inverewe and Kintail, both districts where the cultivation runs up steep slopes, are the only districts where I heard of a tradition of the use of 'slypes' – primitive sledges made of a few boards fixed to a pair of shafts. I think that in most districts the transition was straight from pack-horses to wheeled carts, as I saw it actually happening in some districts from ponies with panniers of peat to motor lorries. Inverewe was also especially instructive to visit because of the descriptions of old life there by Osgood Mackenzie in his *A Hundred Years in the Highlands* and in the reminiscences of Hugh Miller, better known for his work, *The Old Red Sandstone*. Coonie Mitford, whose family was much beloved round Loch Broom, put me up at her house just across the ferry at Ullapool. In collecting, her name was one to conjure with. I also stayed at the friendly hotel at Aultbea and often took the beautiful road to Laide. Alas! When I happened to travel that way years later there was a ring of caravans round the lonely sweep of Gruinard Bay. One is tempted to wonder whether extensive popularisation is the best way to make tourism lucrative to the Highlands themselves.

Laide was the last place that I visited upon my last trip in the spring of 1939. I had moved my collection from Iona to Laggan in the previous autumn so I was able to arrange for what I had collected to be sent straight there in a lorry. I went ahead to prepare for their coming and the kindly tenant of a beautiful old mason-built house with whom I had made friends came with the lorry for the run. We thought so happily of further collecting and more meetings and we little thought of the coming war in a few months and of the changes that it was to bring.

I wish that I had taken more time to find out the history of that obviously very old mason-built house. It represents a great change in the social habits and way of living in the Highlands. In the days when the clans were founded and were growing, the founders of the more important clans and their descendants, the successive chiefs, lived in castles. They also had farms which would have been much more accessible and comfortable, except in moments of stress, and where they would have spent a good deal of time. As time went on and they had many relations settled upon their land, they also had the right of claiming a cuddiche (cuid-oidhche) or night's lodging from such dependants as part of their rent (which would, of course, otherwise be paid in kind). These visits were festive occasions, attended by many ranks of society and afforded patronage that kept alive and maintained the standard of the music and poetry of the Gael.

Upon another trip, I had stayed at Acharacle and, walking over a ridge, had suddenly seen Castle Tioram on an island in Loch Moidart. There are some wooded islands close to the castle that seem to emphasise its apartness from the open countryside and to indicate that it belonged to another age to that in which we live. The ruin of Castle Tioram is almost complete. Looking down at it, it was easy to pick out the different stages such castles went through. It was surrounded by a wall. This had been the original defence, and buildings of slighter construction had been built inside it. In some of these castles, the enclosing wall might go back to the twelfth century. At Castle Sween in Knapdale where I had prowled around, the early enclosing wall can be easily examined. The next stage was the addition of special defences at the entrance. Dunvegan has a very elaborate sea-gate – in the old days it was the only means of access to the castle. It also has a grisly legend of a murder committed there. The following stage was the building of a tower inside the encircling wall. This tower had kitchen and storage rooms below the great hall on the next floor where the chief and his retainers dined, the living quarters were on the floor above. The Exchequer Rolls have very full accounts of the building of such a tower at Tarbert in Knapdale. There were no further modifications to the buildings in Castle Tioram.

In the sixteenth century or perhaps the early seventeenth century, a new style in castles – the building of tower houses – came into fashion. Very fine ones, notably Craigievar Castle, were built just outside the Highland line. An example just within it is Dalcross Castle, close to the airfield. These buildings generally partook more of the nature of a tower than a house and were ornamented with turrets and crenellations that were much copied by Bryce and other architects of the Victorian period. At Dunvegan there was already a fifteenth-century tower but Rory Mór added the Fairy Tower within the outer walls and in the castle house style. It is important to remember that within the tower houses the great hall was still the place where the family of the owner, his guests and his retainers all sat and ate together.

In the seventeenth century, all over Great Britain, the fashion began to spread among the gentry of living in houses with separate dining rooms. Gradually it reached people of less and less standing. By this time, people of position in the Highlands were mingling with the high society of the south. They were not behindhand in adopting the new style of housing, altering their castles if they had them or building mansions. The lesser farmers and tacksmen gradually followed. When the Agricultural Revolution led to the division of the joint farms and new houses were built upon the separately allocated holdings, lime and mortar houses were built upon large farms and then upon lesser ones and this style of building succeeded the local traditional types. The process was patchy. Some individuals as well as some districts lagged behind others. Nor did it always take place directly. There might be a move from a house of couples to one with masonry walls and roof timbers springing from them. One comes across many cases where these survive as byres, while the owner has migrated to a Georgian or later dwelling.

For a large part of the Highlands, the eighteenth century was the era of the stone-mason. Bridges were built for the first time at dangerous fords. Parish churches were not only rebuilt but were slated. Most of the old churches were thatched and there are quite a number of tales of how their roofs were set alight while the congregation was inside by members of an enemy clan. The Mackenzies even have a piobaireachd about such an exploit in their deadly struggle with the MacDonalds of Loch Alsh. When I was collecting about Kyle of Lochalsh I remember reading the gory details of the bitter fighting along that shore.

A good example of the new housing development is a group of cottages at the mouth of Glen Urquhart, built in the time of good Sir James Grant of Grant. The journal of Hugh Miller, a working mason himself, describes his journeys into the western Highlands much in the tone of a venturer into 'Darkest Africa'. I have deliberately recalled this period of house building because it is, for two reasons, important to anyone making a folk museum. In the first place, it emphasises the fact that the styles of the indigenous types of houses in the Highlands were simply evolved to suit local conditions and to use the materials locally available. When other methods of building became available, no distinguishing local feature was retained, no local type persisted.

The second reason, and by far the more important one, is that with more commodious dwellings, the kind of furniture changed. In the houses of the lairds and gentry, built in the styles of architecture known as Queen Anne, Georgian or Regency, the furniture would also be in these successive styles, veneered with mahogany and made by a professional craftsman in Edinburgh or perhaps Perth. But in the museum I had chairs made of plain unpolished wood – one with Queen Anne splat and several definitely Sheraton in style, obviously made by country crafts-men. Most precious of all, in fact the thing that I most treasured in my whole collection, was a home-made chair – the seat a slice cut from a tree-trunk, the legs merely straight bits of tree branches and the back also made from bits of bent branches of trees so carefully matched that they formed the lyre-shaped ornamentation of a chairback in the Empire style. These chairs are a tangible demonstration of the fact that the ranks in society mingled and that there was no peasant style of building or furni-ture in the Highlands any more than there was a peasant dress. The belted plaid and later the kilt were worn by all ranks of society although the quality of the material varied.

I have another outstanding recollection of my travels on the mainland – that of a drive, upon a day of thunder storms, from Ullapool to Inchnadamph. As one went north the moorland with its flat rockfaces looked dark and unfriendly. Stack Polly and Canisp, hills that always look as if they had been produced in a volcanic eruption and not as geologists tell us, by the erosion of the surrounding country, certainly looked that day as if at any moment they would spout flame and molten lava. The flat rock faces upon distant Ben More looked luridly white. There was plenty of thunder but most of the lightning was sheet. One was very much aware that one was sitting in a metal vehicle but put one's trust in the fact that its wheels made contact with the ground by rubber tyres. It was a place in which to recall the betrayal of Montrose, the story of the MacLeods of Assynt and other tragedies that happened not too far from that district. Instead I remember being fascinated by the great Leicester sheep – locally called Lycesters – and in wondering how such large

Above

Dr I. F. Grant in her car with items collected for display at *Am Fasgadh*, including an illicit still in the boot.

HIGHLAND FOLK MUSEUM, KINGUSSIE, 2007

Left

Dr Grant aged 4 years, 1891.

PATRICK GRANT, 2007

Below, left

A somewhat pensive Dr Grant posing for a formal portrait as a young girl.

PATRICK GRANT, 2007

Above

Dr Grant aged 18 on the occasion of being presented at court to King Edward and Queen Alexandra in 1905.

PATRICK GRANT, 2007

Above

Dr Grant at the Great Sphinx, Giza, Egypt in 1935 just having secured ownership of the United Free Church in Iona that was to become the first site for *Am Fasgadh*.

PATRICK GRANT, 2007

Above

Dr Grant with canine companion on Iona with *Am Fasgadh* in the background.

PATRICK GRANT, 2007

Above, right

Dr Grant showing some of the artefacts at *Am Fasgadh*, Iona.

HIGHLAND FOLK MUSEUM,
KINGUSSIE, 2007

Right

Display of artefacts, including a goffering iron on the table, *Am Fasgadh*, Iona.

HIGHLAND FOLK MUSEUM,
KINGUSSIE, 2007

Opposite page, below

The United Free Church in Iona that opened in 1935 as *Am Fasgadh*.

PATRICK GRANT, 2007

Above, left

Display of powder horns, pictures and other items with accompanying explanatory notes above and to the sides at *Am Fasgadh*, Iona.

PATRICK GRANT, 2007

Left

Dresser at Iona showing the Scottish practice of placing the plates sloped forwards which prevents dust from soiling the plates. Also on display on the dresser are Wally dugs.

PATRICK GRANT, 2007

Below, left

Collection at Iona showing a horse collar, creel, butter churns and wooden buckets.

PATRICK GRANT, 2007

Below

Collection of spinning equipment in *Am Fasgadh*, Iona, including a spinning jack on the left used to wind yarn, as well as a spinning wheel to the right.

PATRICK GRANT, 2007

Above, right

Church at Laggan that became the second siting of *Am Fasgadh* in 1938.

HIGHLAND FOLK MUSEUM, KINGUSSIE, 2007

Right

Dr Grant outside the Manse at Laggan.

HIGHLAND FOLK MUSEUM, KINGUSSIE, 2007

Below

Household utensils in *Am Fasgadh* Highland Museum, Laggan.

HIGHLAND FOLK MUSEUM, KINGUSSIE, 2007

Above

Pitmain Lodge, Kingussie, the third siting of *Am Fasgadh* from 1944.

HIGHLAND FOLK MUSEUM, KINGUSSIE, 2007

Left

Dr Grant outside Pitmain Lodge, Kingussie.

HIGHLAND FOLK MUSEUM, KINGUSSIE, 2007

Below, left

Display at *Am Fasgadh*, Kingussie showing a range of domestic furniture, including cradles, as well as a number of wall clocks.

HIGHLAND FOLK MUSEUM, KINGUSSIE, 2007

Above

Display of kitchen-related items at Kingussie, including a number of chains with hooks for holding cooking pots.

Right

Postcard of a 'General View of Cottages, The Highland Folk Museum, Kingussie'.

Below, right

Collection of buildings at *Am Fasgadh*, Kingussie *c.*1954.

Above, left

Dr Grant on the occasion of
receiving an honorary degree
of Doctor of Letters from the
University of Edinburgh
in 1948.

PATRICK GRANT, 2007

Above, right

Colonel Hugh Gough
Grant CB, Dr Grant's father.

PATRICK GRANT, 2007

Left

Field Marshal Sir Patrick
Grant, Goldstick-in-Waiting to
Queen Victoria, Governor of
Chelsea Hospital and Dr
Grant's grandfather.

PATRICK GRANT, 2007

Below, left

Grant family picnic
at Balnespick, July 1936,
Dr Grant second from right.

PATRICK GRANT, 2007

animals could pick up a living upon that moorland when at home the little black-faced sheep find this hard enough. The answer no doubt is geological and in the quality of the grazing.

This trip was not the furthest north that I went. I heard that there was an antique shop in Thurso, which stocked some of the things I was after. It was interesting to drive north through Caithness with its fences and old cottages of flagstones – but that of course was not Highland territory.

11

West and East

A FTER the spring of 1939 circumstances prevented further
expeditions on the same scale as those that I had made to
the north western coast and the islands. The War broke out and
then I had the burden, physical and financial, of running the
museum upon a more demanding scale at Kingussie. I very much
regret that lack of money and time did not allow me to visit some
of the other islands such as Eigg and Coll and to make a serious
collecting trip to Barra. I am also sorry that I was not able to re-
visit Kintyre and Knapdale.

What did survive in the south west far better than did the
'coupled' type of house of the central Highlands was the local
style of building. The marked difference that distinguished it was
obviously due to the kind of local stone which was mainly of a
laminated type, in contrast to the knobbly kinds of the rest of
the Highlands. The houses were rectangular, with gable ends.
But, as I have already noted, there was not a chimney flue in
these gables and the hearth and, later on, the fireplaces were
built against a partition, and were in the middle of the house. I
looked at all the ruined cottages that I could find and found
evidence that this was so. I rather stress the point because the
double walls of a chimney flue in the gable end of a ruined
cottage stand up to the weather very well. All over the Highlands
they abound and it is interesting to remember that they belong
to a later period, after the Agricultural Revolution.

During the years before the War, besides my trips to the north
west, I was able to manage shorter visits to Easter Ross and to

Perthshire. Mrs Macrae was the wife of Macrae, the Keeper at Balnespick, and a beloved and faithful friend of my family. Her home had been in Easter Ross and under her wing I took two most rewarding trips to her old haunts but I have already noted a sad disappointment at Evanton. I also stayed at Castle Leod at Strathpeffer and visited an area where the linen industry had once flourished. There did not seem to be any surviving implements but I learned a good deal. It was a great joy to visit this area, the most fertile in the whole of the Highlands, especially just after having seen the tenacious struggle to live off the land that had to be endured in many other areas. All about one were the distant hills. Southwards lay a rampart to which the changing seasons and the fitful weather gave unending variation of colour and sometimes even the appearance of height. Northwards, the top of Ben Wyvis looked rather disappointingly flat. (It was a youthful dream of mine that by some means its steep sides would be continued to make a beautiful conical peak far higher than Ben Nevis, the highest mountain in the British Isles and, hopefully, even to out-top Mont Blanc.) In spite of his shape he generally hangs on to a bit of his mantle of snow long after most other Highland hills – a fact of which the 'winter-sporters' or those who exploit their activities are barely beginning to take advantage. Beyond his shoulder a magnificent cluster of peaks is revealed. One is looking at these hills from not much above the sea level of the Firths of Moray and of Cromarty. Against such a background the fine agriculture of the Black Isle and of the coast beyond takes on a special quality. The splendid crops and livestock, the well-built farm houses and steadings and the look of prosperity of the people were in such happy contrast to all that one had seen and learnt of Highland conditions. It is an enjoyable luxury to indulge oneself in a 'good hate', and the strongest reason for mine of the Highlands and Islands Development Board, is that because the Cromarty Firth is exceptionally deep and a convenient landing place, the best agricultural region in the Highlands (and even less good ones are distressingly rare) should be industrialised. They ignore the empty sea lochs of the west, set in a sterile countryside and deep enough to hold the greatest battleships of the British Navy as they actually did in the last War. To spare our best land and to bring some activity to some of our worst, only needed a road across an area not very wide and with a number of passes. The drovers took their cattle through it. In fact, it seems a pity that our engineering experts are not as canny as old General Wade who mainly followed old routes when he made his famous roads. It might be remembered that the old drovers brought their traditional droving tracks to the head of the Beauly Firth and straight south. If the Highlands and Islands Development Board had not chosen to industrialise the land round the Cromarty Firth, the main road north might have gone the same way. It would hardly, I suspect, have equalled the cost and difficulty in making the Kessock Bridge.

The differences in the lay-out of the land and of the distribution of the population can also be accounted for by comparatively recent historical and economic reasons, but the differences between the western and eastern Highlands are older and subtler. During the power politics of the sixteenth and seventeenth centuries, Argyll was dominant in the west and Huntly in the east, and it may be noted that while publicly Argyll was the stronger, when they met at the head of their forces at the Battle of Glenlivet, Huntly's men soon fought their way up the slope and defeated him even although Argyll had taken up a stronger position on rising ground. Earlier than that, the great Lords of the Isles, for all their efforts, never succeeded in permanently influencing the eastern Highlands. It is true that Anglo-Norman influences introduced by Malcolm Canmore's line of kings spread more or less evenly over the mainland, but earlier, although the coastal lands of the Laich of Moray and the Black Isle are far more fertile than is most of the west, the Norse never colonised them or produced a mixed race – the Gall-Gaidheal – as they did in the west. It is true, also, that the culture of the

Scots Gaels submerged that of the Picts all over the Highlands, but it may not be fanciful to recall that in prehistoric times there were two separate cultures – that of the builders of the chambered cairns coming from the south west and that of the Beaker Folk from the north east. A trifling but curious survival of the differences between the western and eastern Highlands is in the attitudes of old-fashioned Highlanders to the meat of pigs. When I was a child, the local people in eastern Inverness-shire did not keep pigs and pork, bacon, *etc*, had not the same popularity as elsewhere. The Boar's Stone at Inverness illustrates that the boar was a Pictish totem. The Gaels, however, were particularly addicted to eating roasted boars at their feasts and to hunting them. In an agricultural report on Lewis the large number of pigs kept and their savage nature was commented upon.

At the present day, when old traditions have almost faded away and local distinctions been obliterated, if one travels about much in the eastern and the western Highlands and Islands one becomes aware that the local people have a definite sense of the differences between East and West Coasters. I think myself that this has a more ancient pedigree than a good many of the later fashionably 'folksy' tales.

12
Perthshire and Angus

DURING the autumn and winter I had occasion to do some collecting in Perthshire. But I did it in a different way. It is against all traditions of Highland loyalty to the homes of one's ancestors to admit that I think Perthshire is the most satisfying district in the Highlands. Its hills are high and shapely, its timber fine and varied, its agricultural land fertile. I spent the happiest months of my whole life staying as a child of eight in a house on Loch Tummel that an uncle had rented. Ever since, my vision of an 'earthly paradise' is of Schiehallion with a loch and perhaps open woodland where one could identify the trees and not the dense planting of scots pines as I remember it at its feet. In this 'earthly paradise' of my imagining there would also be a hive of busily buzzing drone bumble bees, far-fetched as such an idea would seem to a naturalist. The reason for this is that having found some discarded drone bumble bees clinging wet and numb to some flowers after a shower of rain, I got an up-turned box and arranged them on some flowers in its shelter. I was a child of the Victorian era and when I asked for something to hold the flowers, I was not told the macabre facts of life of a bumble bee byke but, as a good little girl who was being kind to the less fortunate, I was praised and given an empty jam-jar. I went on collecting fresh flowers and more drone bumble bees. I was stung by a working bee that most reprehensibly was taking time off (to be honest, a bumble bee's sting hurts much less than that of a honey bee) but that did not stop me. Evidently Providence, having destined me for the job of making a folk museum, instituted in me an innate tendency for collecting discarded objects regardless of the cost.

In later years, the part of Perthshire that was familiar to me was that which one saw driving north or south. It was an enjoyable drive in the days before the road was cluttered up with lorries and caravans. Besides being beautiful to the eye, the district was stimulating to the mind because of its associations. Blair Atholl was a key position from which to control the central Highlands and tales about its successive owners, especially about the Wolf of Badenoch and his disreputable family, make colourful reading. Upon one of the rising grounds where the valley widens just before one comes to it, Montrose raised the Royal standard at the outset of his campaign. When I was writing *In the Tracks of Montrose*, I spent the best part of a summer's day trying to identify the exact place. In the later campaign of Bonnie Dundee (Graham of Claverhouse) upon almost the same ground, in the Battle of Killiecrankie (1689), the government troops under General Mackay were drawn up very much where the old road ran, and the Highlanders were massed upon the low hills. Mackay was faced with the decision of whether to extend his line or shorten and strengthen it. He decided wrongly and when the Highlanders charged downhill in the new battle tactic that Montrose had so brilliantly exploited, they broke his line. The victory, however, was a barren one. Dundee was killed in it and the Rising fizzled out ignominiously.

The look of the countryside during the centuries cannot have changed much because it was still being tilled in an archaic fashion when, from eighteenth century travellers' accounts and maps, we do know pretty well what it looked like. The strath of the Garry had a wide marshy bottom and upon the lower slopes were the irregular patches of cultivation and the clusters of joint-tenants' houses such as I have already described in Strathdearn. The houses were made with couples and by fortunate chance one single shed built in the way actually survives. Even now, on the way north, I notice a subtle change in the lay-out of the buildings and general look of the farms when one is within a few miles of Dunkeld (where incidentally one is crossing the old Highland Line). It is not only my imagination for other people have commented upon it to me and it is probably due to physical conditions. But for years after the '45, according to the accounts of people who came this way, it was about here that they passed into a different civilisation. Everyone wore Highland dress and Gaelic was spoken. Then within not more than half a century the agricultural reforms had drained the wide bottom of the Strath and turned it and the lower slopes of the hills into an orderly pattern of well-cultivated fields that, with little modification, is as we see it at the present day.

Meanwhile, the appearance, manners and customs of the people changed. The women no longer took immense pains to dye the wool in the colours of their tartan nor did they actually spin it. Linen was no longer made. Boughten cloth and cotton fabrics replaced the homelier stuffs. The hand-loom weaver disappeared but at Pitlochry there is a survival of the small, water-driven woollen mills that, for a time, took the place of the domestic industry in the Highlands. The itinerant tailor no longer made a stay in house after house and the traditional epic tales that he and every other wandering craftsman, musician or traveller were expected to recount, have long gone out of date.

Those changes had happened and all about that part of the road as I knew it in my youth before the First World War and even through the uncertainty of the period between the Wars there was a feeling of stability about the land. Even after the last War, although one saw the crops harvested into bales and the kind of livestock in the fields had changed and the fields were cultivated by tractors, the quality of the land ensured that it received the same careful cultivation.

Curiously enough, in spite of this stability, a kind of mechanisation did begin very early upon this good land. As I passed the larger farm steadings I was intrigued to notice rounded buildings and learnt that they were threshing mills worked by horse-power. I am not mechanically minded and such farm-steads are exceptional to and not typical of the Highlands so I did not investigate. Another mechanical installation to be found on largish farms and that I actually saw in Aberdeenshire was a fanner (to separate the chaff from the grain) that was turned by a handle. There was an ill-natured story that upon one of the rare occasions when fisherfolk came to a farm they were told that the fanner was an organ and that it would play a tune if they turned the handle. This story illustrates the division between the east coast fishermen who formed a separate community and the west coast crofter-fishermen. I gather that the distinction between the fishers and the landward people diminished as one went northwards but it used to be said of Nairn that it must be the largest town in the world because different languages were spoken at either end – of course, referring to the Scots-speaking people of the fishertown and the Gaelic-speaking country folk.

As our road began the long upward gradient to Drumochter the effects of the Agricultural Depression that began in the second half of the nineteenth century became more and more apparent as one came to poorer, bleaker land. Fields that had been reclaimed became unremunerative to cultivate and reverted to rough pasture. On the other hand, as we approached the grouse moors, one saw evidence of a most valuable source of money, employment and social stimulus that became of real importance about the middle of the nineteenth century (a most welcome corrective to the Agricultural Depression) and flourished until the First World War, survived during the inter-war period and is now suffering from a decline. I refer of course to grouse shooting, especially when grouse driving came into fashion. The large shooting lodges can easily be dated; many of them show by turrets or other devices the influence of Bryce and the Victorian Gothic style. In my mind's eye a drive up that road provided the background of a gigantic and most beautiful folk museum. I was able to attend a roup upon one of my drives along it and I made a most welcome purchase. This was called a 'dolly' and was used for washing blankets. It consisted of a number of pegs at the end of a pole, which was used to thump the blankets in the tub. According to old accounts girls used to wash the blankets by treading them with their bare feet either in the burn or in a tub. They used to 'kilt up their coaties' a bit in the process and the pictures of these girls at work gave the coarsely minded a certain pleasure. I was once rung up and asked if I had such a picture in my collection. The enquiring man wished to reproduce one in some publication he was devising as a travel attraction in order, as he said, 'to amuse the tourists'. He got a flea in his ear instead of a picture. So I was very glad to demonstrate in my collection that other methods of washing blankets were also used. One of the penalties of running the museum was having to endure the comments of some Lowland Scots. One old boy who 'toddled' round at a gait that, as Sir Walter Scott pointed out, is very characteristic of some sections of Lowland middle-class Scots, remarked at intervals, 'How entertaining'. I grumbled about this to a friend but the only reply I got was, 'I do admire that man's temerity'.

I visited one excellent antique dealer at Aberfeldy who fully entered into the spirit of my search and among other things sold me an iron cooking pot said to have belonged to a character in local tales, the 'Lady of Lawers'. It had obviously been made by a different method to the usual old iron cooking utensils from old cottages and I am sure was genuinely older.

Perth did not become a nightmare of congested motor traffic until some time after I had to give up my car. By the riverside there were some dealers in discarded objects – one would not name them in the same breath as Love and some other well-known Perth antique dealers. I bought several things from them. I got a dish with an unusual blue pattern upon it. I have only seen similar ones in the western Highlands. It had no maker's mark on it but I was told that a German ship used to visit the western Highlands to sell a cargo of china and I think that this may have been a specimen. My most important port of call was to a scrap-iron merchant at Scone. Among other things I was able to get examples of the use people who live in areas with flat stones (in contrast to the jagged ones of the north) would put them to in making stands for bee-skeps and troughs for hen food. The whole of my life as a collector rubbed into my mind the importance of local supplies of material in determining the nature of the country people's crafts.

I owe my acquaintance with the yard of the 'scrappy' at Scone to Lady Maitland. I owe her a great deal besides. We met when we both happened to be staying at the same hotel in Edinburgh. We did not take long to discover that we followed the same unusual pursuit. Jean Maitland had an extraordinary intimate knowledge and love of the rural life of Angus and had begun to try to collect the homely things that she saw were so rapidly disappearing, with the hope that an Angus Folk Museum would some day be set up. She was able to keep them in the very large dairy and back-premises of her home at Burnside to await the appearance of the suitable premises and organisation that she hoped for. Years went by and she had many disappointments but at last the perfect site became available in the shape of a row of cottages at Glamis and an organisation was formed that would give the collection continuity of care. She had an exhaustive knowledge of all the 'scrappies' and shops of the rag and bone variety in the south east and she was most generous in passing on to me the names of likely dealers. She seemed to know every old cottage and its contents within most of Angus. She taught me a lot. For instance, it was she who pointed out that during the Napoleonic Wars and for a few years afterwards laburnum wood was used to replace the mahogany veneer on furniture and that laburnum trees were planted for this use. There was actually a wood of them at Burnside. Laburnum wood is easy to recognise – it is curiously variegated in light and dark streaks and it has a coarse grain and an almost greasy-looking appearance.

I enjoyed staying at Burnside and going with her on forays. The only snag was that she had much sharper eyes than I had. A sad case was a wooden mousetrap that she instantly detected in a mass of junk. I really coveted that grimy little object but would have hated to let her feel under any obligation to give it up to her guest. I broke the Tenth Commandment for a long time before I got a mousetrap like that one. Her friendship bolstered up my self-esteem in a more important way. She was a woman in a very good position, a wife, the mother of a family, mistress of a 'Big Hoose'. It was pleasant, as a rather dowdy nobody, to share with her what most of my closer contacts considered a regrettable eccentricity.

13
Workers in Wood and Iron

O F course I have seen from childhood that trees grew very well in many parts of the Highlands. As a well-brought-up little Grant I took pride in seeing the splendid fir trees in Strathspey, for pine is the badge of my clan. I also was used to hearing descriptions of the treeless conditions of the Western Isles. Later on I learnt of the abundance of scrub in parts of the west and that in the seventeenth and eighteenth centuries some iron ore had been imported to a few places for smelting and then exporting as pig-iron. It would be interesting to know how far the greater availability of iron in Norway, in view of possible counter-balancing disadvantages, affected the social environment. When I visited Oslo I saw examples of the very distinctive Norwegian style of building wooden churches, but I have never come across an analysis of the effects of the more extensive use of iron ore upon Norwegian as compared to Highland agriculture. It was not until I started to collect for my museum that I realised how very, very precious iron had been in the Highlands.

Apart from the derivation of iron from 'bog ore' which, I believe, was attempted but never became a widespread practice and from haematitic ore occasionally mined at a few sites such as the Lecht in Upper Banffshire, all iron had to be imported and, of course, paid for. When I was collecting, it was interesting to find that from the appearance of an exhibit I could often form a good idea of the fertility of the district from which it came. The most handsome and weighty chains for hanging the cooking pot over the fire came from the areas with good land. All the attractive bannock turners and the elegant girdles were specially characteristic of Perthshire and Strathspey. The use of two bits of wood with pegs in between in place of an iron pot chain was evidently the sign of dire poverty. Other substitutes were used for iron or even for wood. Leather was used for hinges for shutters and doors and probably in the old days doors were made to turn on wooden pivots. On the Long Island sometimes, wood, so precious itself, was used instead of iron as, for instance, in door fastenings. I was anxious to obtain a specimen and at last saw a door with a very ingenious contraption in a roofless cottage that had lately been abandoned. I asked the man who was kindly acting as my guide whom the cottage belonged to so that I could get that door. He replied that it had belonged to his auntie who 'had passed on'. I said that surely she had left her things to someone and he replied, 'To me'. I said in that case would he sell me the door but he demurred, saying that it was his auntie's. I pointed out that she had 'passed' and he was her heir, the door was his and would he not let me buy it. He still hesitated and I suggested that he might have a nice text carved on her tombstone if he let me buy the door fastening. That clinched the matter and I got the fastening, although I think that he can only have had a very brief text inscribed with the sum that I gave him.

The utmost use had to be made of any wood that there was. When I visited the Islands, ponies and creels were still very much used for such work as carrying peat or seaweed, although wheeled vehicles and even motor lorries were taking their place. It was easy to acquire wooden pack-saddles and they were made of several pieces of wood nailed together. They were not very old. I was lucky enough to be given a very old pack-saddle from Perthshire where, of course, wood was plentiful. It was made of solid blocks of wood carved into shape. When substitutes for iron articles had to be so freely used, I feel surprised that something was not devised to take the place of cruisies.

Books about archaeology tell of the Iron Age. Kipling, in his *Rewards and Fairies*, makes evident a salient effect, which was that the possession of iron tools gave man mastery over the forests and enabled him to fell the trees. In some ways the Highlands, up to the eighteenth century, had not advanced very far from an early stage of Iron Age evolution. During the Middle Ages, the blacksmiths had produced swords, chain-mail and iron caps like those current elsewhere, but the craftsmanship had died out with the use of more sophisticated weapons, although the tradition that they had these ancient skills still lingered in some families. I did not enquire and unfortunately did not happen to come across any information of a local Highland blacksmith making one of the basket-hilted swords that became the characteristic weapon – the Highland sword – in the seventeenth century. Local Highland tools for workaday purposes only seem to have been capable of hacking and splitting. When I was collecting I was several times given heads of adzes and axes but no other wood-working tools. Axes, of course, are still very much in use. Living in the country one does not normally have an adze, but a saw, a hammer and a screw-driver with nails and screw-nails, a gimlet and an axe. The use the last item is generally put to is splitting wood to make fire-kindlings – a job I was very bad at! (To make a complete diversion – one day on a collecting trip, I saw a stretch of moorland that had been burnt and I commented to the woman who was with me how forlorn the burnt stems of the heather looked. She replied briskly that they were grand for kindlings and that one of the jobs that she had had to do as a child was to go out and gather a supply of them.) At first in collecting I assumed that people had had such tools and thrown them away when they were worn out but then I realised they had never possessed them. They cut with an axe or adze. They also obviously pared the rough wood. The most obvious simple tool would be a spoke-shave but there is no Gaelic word for this. Visitors to the workshop of a modern maker of woodwork by early methods, have described how skilfully the adze could be used and the beautiful surfaces produced. No doubt the dirk which was constantly carried could also be turned to good account. An iron rod could be used for boring. But to make staved vessels that were watertight with only an adze is more difficult to envisage.

Very heavy timber was seldom used. In old castles one does see flooring planks that had been cut from a section of the middle of a tree trunk, the sides having been split off by means of an adze (generally smaller trees that were naturally growing quite straight or with the right bend, as for instance for the couples used in the central Highlands housing style, to suit the purpose for which they were required). I was once rebuked for not realising this. As I had totally failed to secure an old sled or slype, I decided to ask a local man, who remembered seeing one, to make a replica. He asked me what I thought was rather a stiff price for nailing a few short planks across the end of two long bits of wood but he remarked it was not the wood or fixing it together that took the skill and the time but the finding of them. The couples and the other roof timbers were fixed together by means of wooden pegs and I am sure that the holes into which they were fixed were made by burning with a red-hot iron rod, as was evidently done in the primitive furniture. When I built the Lewis cottage in the museum grounds at Kingussie, I got an old man who had settled not far away to direct the building of it as he remembered his old home, but he insisted upon using nails to fasten the timber because wooden fastenings had gone out long before his time. 'Deals', as they were called, planks sawn at the local watermills, had also become available in many districts from about the middle of the eighteenth century. The old houses were primitive but there was no housing shortage because everyone, with his neighbour's help, could gather the materials and build one for himself. I remember there was a great post-War building scheme at Newtonmore and work was held up when the iron gutters for the houses were not delivered. At that moment, Mr MacDonald was putting the finishing touches to the roof of the Inverness-shire cottage at *Am Fasgadh* by arranging a fringe of heather at the edge of the thatching to carry the drips clear of the walls. Chairs and stools were most ingeniously contrived out of naturally straight, forked or bent branches. Of course, the furniture that I was able to collect was only the survivals, used by people in very poor circumstances, of what had been the general fashion. A very touching feature was the number of children's chairs. How backward in the use of wood-working tools the Highlanders were is well illustrated by the account book of Inverness bailie John Steuart, published by the Scottish History Society. It is well known that there was a considerable export of herrings and salmon to the Continent, but it is from these letters one learns that there was a considerable import to Inverness from Rotterdam, Hamburg and other parts, of wooden staves for herring and salmon barrels and of iron bands for them. Planks were also imported. I have already described the old wooden plough which had only the minimum of iron and the cabar lar and cas chrom or foot plough which were made of a naturally-shaped shaft of wood with an iron blade affixed to the end.

The style of thatching in the Outer Hebrides resembled that used for a stack of corn. The straw was laid loose on the roof and secured by a complicated and symmetrical arrangement of rope or, in recent times, by herring nets. Invariably the thatch was renewed every year (incidentally, the old thatch was thriftily used as fertiliser). When I built my little Lewis house after I moved the Folk Museum to Kingussie of course it was duly thatched in the traditional way. An assistant stood on each side of the cottage and, having fastened a stone to the end of the rope, tossed it over the roof to the man on the other side who weighted it with a stone to keep it in place and then threw it back and the rope was thus tossed backwards and forwards till the whole of the roof was securely roped. When I had to renew the thatch I found that not only was straw expensive but I could only procure it in a bale and threshed by machinery and the stalks were bent, split, broken and not very durable for thatching. So I decided to make my own straw. I sowed a little rye (which is said to make the toughest straw), had it cut and then, with improvised flails, we threshed it. One of the men engaged for this job said he 'had heard tell' of the possibility of an unpractised thresher getting a crack on the head. Great care was taken that no such accident happened. The rye was threshed. The grain was appreciated by my livestock. The cottage was re-thatched. Unfortunately the unskilled threshers had left some grain in the ears of rye which the jackdaws, in other ways a regular pest, discovered and disturbed the thatch in pecking it out. To discourage them I tied rags to little sticks and stuck them into the cottage roof. I had a stream of enquiries from visitors asking if this were an ancient Gaelic custom for warding off ghoulies and ghosties.

To return to the consideration of flails. The two pieces of wood of which they are made are joined in two different ways – either (a) a leather thong is passed through a hole bored at the end of the back of the bits of wood (to be precise the swingle-pole and the striker) or (b) a connecting thong or bit of rope is tied round the end of each piece of wood, being kept in place by a shallow channel cut round the wood. I was greatly interested to find that nearly all my flails with the (b) fastenings came from places with names of Norse derivation; as a matter of fact they came from the Islands. I wondered if this indicated that the style of making them was an ancient Norse tradition. This was an exciting idea. In spite of the fact that according to all the accounts of them that I read, the language and customs of the people of the Islands were wholly Gaelic, one wondered if some little custom had survived in the form of flails. I learned otherwise. In the (a) type, all the 'swingle poles' were carefully shaped and were of good timber, according to an expert mostly of ash which is a particularly tough sort of wood. The 'strikers' which were the parts of the flail most apt to be broken, were generally of hazel which grows all over the country and from which straight rounded pieces of wood could be easily cut. The (b) type of flail that comes from the Islands and the west was made of straight pieces of wood of no particular kind. In one case, the striker was only a bit of rope. As hazel, let alone ash, does not grow in the districts that they come from, it is pretty obvious that the accessibility of supply of the material was the dominant factor.

Another example of traditional variation due to local supply is that of the peat spade. Peat varies in quality. In Lewis it is hard to cut and is cut into long narrow blocks, and for doing so a spade with a long flange is used. In some districts it is soft and is cut into thicker cubes and the spade has a short flange. I had about 18 different peat spades and men who visited the museum invariably picked out the one from their own locality as the handiest. I always made a point of asking them.

A great variety of wooden utensils for the home and dairy were made, sometimes with a knife, sometimes evidently upon a lathe. In my *Highland Folk Ways* I quoted Osgood Mackenzie's description of milking the cows and how the wooden milk dishes were washed by filling them with cold water, lighting a fire and dropping in very hot pebbles. Some of my dishes showed marks of burning.

Apart from crudely made jars that I was told were used for holding oil, there seems to have been little attempt to use the local clay except at Barvas in Lewis. I used to know a Mrs Quiggin who was the widow of one of the pioneers in the scholarly study of the Gaelic language and who had stayed at Barvas and had seen the pottery being made. It was always done by the women, who kneaded the pots into shape, dipped them in milk and baked them on the fire. In her day, the women were making tea-sets for sale to the tourists. They were very crude and most breakable articles. I am indebted to Mr Hugh Cheape for telling me that shards of pottery baked in the same fashion have been found in early and medieval sites in the Highlands. Some of the jars were skilfully shaped. It is evident that, as in so many other cases, as the use of more convenient or more socially acceptable kinds of containers spread, the old crafts died. For instance I was always told that the tinkers did a great trade in colourful bowls from Lowland potteries exchanged for rabbit skins.

The problem of the making of the churns, milk cogs, cheesers and all the other staved vessels still troubles me. All these were in constant use although I have been told that butter could be made by shaking milk in a leather bag. Making them was evidently not carried on as a local craft because in the many accounts of parishes in the Old Statistical Account that I have read, there is never a mention of a wood-worker of any kind in the list of local craftsmen. They may have been bought at the local town or they more probably were made by wandering cairds – the ancestors of the tinkers – who certainly carved dirk handles, did metal-work and made horn spoons. Especially in later times they may have carried a portable lathe, but more probably they relied upon the adze and even with the most skilful use it would have been difficult to make a watertight fit between the staves. It implies that a very ancient and skilful craft was widely used. Some of the finer, smaller vessels are most skilfully made. Besides containing bands, the separate staves are 'feathered', that is, by small slits they are interlocked to each other. It is an ancient craft, for early silver quaichs made in Inverness in the seventeenth century are engraved to look like the wooden vessels and have the patterning. Old Highland silver quaichs are real collectors' pieces and I could not hope to acquire one for *Am Fasgadh*. What I did hope very much to get, and diligently asked for wherever I went, was a wooden quaich with carved handles, modern examples of which are much sold in tourist shops. On my first collecting trip to the Long Island, when I was staying at Creagorry, I made the usual enquiry and I was asked did I mean a sugar bowl and a bowl, gaily painted in black, red and gold, was produced and I was told that the fisher-folk had got it when they had gone to Wick or Orkney to work at the herring fishing. I met with these bowls again and again and always when there were herring fishermen in the family. Sometimes they were called 'Riga' bowls and they were obviously of Russian origin.

The people were ingenious in finding substitutes for wood and in turning local things to good account in other ways. Heather used to be made into rope for holding on the thatch in the Outer Islands but it has long since been replaced by coir ropes. The tough bent grass of the Islands was made into horse-collars, the saddle-cloth under a pack-saddle, chair seats and bowls that could be used to hold dry substances. I got good specimens of all these things. I have been told that stiff docken stems were sometimes used as the uprights for a creel. I was told that in the old days wickerwork was used for doors. In the north-west where scrub wood was abundant, wickerwork was used a great deal more. I have already told the sad tale of how I missed my one chance of getting a door of wickerwork. It is a most perishable substance and in collecting and arranging one was always up against the problem that whereas iron was durable and expensive and very carefully kept, supplies for wickerwork were on the spot. Few tools were required to work it, and speci-mens were all too fragile and tasty for woodworms. All over the Highlands it was used with a coating of clay for indoor parti-tions and also for creels and baskets for gathering potatoes. But in the west it was used a great deal more widely. Wickerwork panels were built into the walls of barns to provide ventilation and it was even used for complete buildings. On the way to Kyle of Lochalsh, close to the road, there was a barn almost completely made of it. On my comings and goings I saw it disin-tegrate and had not the means to save it. When, as the result of improvements in housing, better furniture came into use, wickerwork was introduced as panels in cupboards. I was told many times that at one time coffins were made of it. I mentioned that it is worthwhile writing of them more fully. I had been surprised to notice that water-worn round pebbles were embedded in the cement in the main aisle in Iona Cathedral and

I asked a man who had helped in the restoration work why this was so. He replied that when the workmen opened the crypt they found a quantity of skeletons in the remains of wicker coffins and beside each of them a handful of these pebbles. The veneration for such pebbles takes one back to times before the Iron Age. They were found in Neolithic burial cairns, and there is evidence of the survival of the belief till the present time. Much larger ones have always lain upon the grave slab in Rothiemurchus churchyard of Shaw, who led Clan Cay in the fight on the Inches at Perth. It is said that a curse would lie upon anyone who removed them. When I had the museum I was always terrified that someone would present it with some relic with a similar malediction attached to it. The roots of our feelings and beliefs go back a very long way.

14
Other Crafts

A S I think over my collecting days and the things I managed
to get, I feel that I did not sufficiently differentiate between
the work of two different groups of craftsmen. To take the later
group briefly first, there were the craftsmen of what I think of
as the Second Iron Age – the masons who built the bridges over
which the roads ran that were to carry in the new tools which, to
my mind, made this new age in the Highlands. There were also
the carpenters and joiners of the mason-built homes of the gentry
and farmers on the newly demarcated separate farms. It was they
who, with the new tools, very notably with the saw, made the
fittings for their houses and furniture. These craftsmen served
wider areas than a parish and tended to live in the new villages
being built in many parts of the Highlands. At the same period
or rather later, and even more typical of the greatest social development of the age – the Industrial Revolution – went the use of
water-power for purposes other than grinding grain: the little local
mills for scutching flax, fulling cloth, and perhaps a little later,
spinning and weaving, sawing timber and many other purposes.

As part of its ancient economy, however, an earlier group of
more closely localised craftsmen were already to be found in the
Highlands long before the group described above. The (Old)
Statistical Accounts of the parishes of Scotland give lists of
them. The proportions of the workers in the various callings are
remarkably similar. In the Parish of Alvie, for example, there
were two smiths, six weavers, four tailors and two 'brog' (ie
brogue) makers. As entries relating to these workers occur

frequently in the account book written between 1769 and 1782
by my great-great-great-grandfather, of which I made a careful
study for my *Every-Day Life on an Old Highland Farm*, I feel
that I have a general idea of such people's circumstances. They
all, except for some millers, rented a small piece of land and
obviously partly subsisted upon it, although they occasionally
had to buy some extra grain. All of them except the smiths did
seasonal jobs, such as harvest work. It is the proportion of the
different callings and the absence of wood-workers and of
potters (such a favourite present day handicraft) that seems to
be so surprising but it is quite typical of those times. In all the
many descriptions of individual parishes in the accounts that I
have read I never came across the mention of these craftsmen in
the lists, although I specially looked out for it. Not included
among the craftsmen and working for a wider area than the
parish was the meal miller. Under the old rights of astriction,
tenants had to grind their grain at the landlord's mill, and
because of this the miller was not always a very popular figure.

Among the local craftsmen the smith had earlier on been
most important as the maker and repairer of the earlier form of
body armour. The word 'gowan', a place-name, is a corruption
of the Gaelic word for smith ('gobha') and indicates the piece of
land allocated to him by virtue of his office. I have mentioned a
few of the things that he made, such as cruisies and cooking-pot
chains. He also made the grates, so important when the hearth
was moved from the centre of the room, and the fire-tongs – you
treated a peat fire with respect and moved the peats with the
tongs, you never poked it. In every parish on a salmon river, he
made the forks used for the illegal practice of 'burning water' –
that is spearing the salmon after attracting them to the surface
by a lighted torch. He of course also shod the horses and he has
continued to do so and to mend the newly introduced farm
implements long after the other local craftsmen have gone. I had
a little wooden harrow which I collected on the Long Island. Its
teeth had been hammered out of old horseshoes.

There were always comparatively few shoe (brogue) makers. People's shoes were made of undressed leather and without soles or welts. They evidently often made them for themselves, but a farm servant's wages included the provision of a pair of shoes per year. I did not have the triumph of including a pair of brogues in my museum, but judging from a very ancient set of cobbler's tools from Wester Ross I was able to obtain, the later, more conventional type of craftsman quite early took over shoe-making.

In all the lists of craftsmen in a parish, the number of tailors was surprisingly large. In such a 'do it yourself' kind of society, to make and mend one's clothes would seem a comparatively simple job. No doubt the scarcity of needles and scissors had something to do with it. One has to remember that in England in the old days pins were so expensive that the allowance to a married woman of the small sums that she made by some work of her own, such as poultry-keeping on a farm, was termed her 'pin-money'. The daughter-in-law of the old man who kept the Account Book had to send specially to Inverness for 'spigs', small headless nails, so needles would have been very expensive and hard to come by. According to an old Gaelic poem, hen's feathers were used in the stitching upon brogues. Shears, which are much simpler than scissors, were sufficiently important possessions to be carved upon west Highland tombstones. One is tempted to wonder if, before the opening up of the Highlands in the later part of the eighteenth century, the women did much sewing. Their principal garment was the plaid and the married women's head-dress was the linen-cloth fastened round the head. I had a quantity of mutches and in one's memories of the old countrywomen, they looked so trim in their snow-white caps as they went about the house and the byre, but all the mutches in my collection were of cotton fabric and one wonders if the fashion for elaborate caps had come down the social scale like so much else. The goffering irons of which I had a quantity, like nearly all the cooking pots, obviously dated from the cast iron period.

Old pictures show that with the belted plaid or the kilt, the doublet was elaborately made with much ornamentation. But lesser people whose portraits were not painted also took pride in their appearance. Stewart of Garth wrote that the country people would willingly submit to 'personal privation in regard to food and accommodation in order to procure arms and habiliments which may set off to advantage a person unbent and unsubdued by conscious inferiority …'. When riding, trews instead of the belted plaid were worn. They fitted the feet and legs closely and must have been difficult garments to put on and still more to make. One picture, and I think others, shows that the hose were of stuff and not knitted. All Highlanders wore the belted plaid or the kilt. In all essentials the Highlanders' clothes were the same and there was no peasant dress, not one which it was a prerog-ative to wear. Actual textiles themselves as well as the clothes that they were made into were important to the Highlander and it is not surprising to find that in every parish there were a number of weavers. The horizontal loom but not the fly-shuttle had evidently come into general use comparatively early. I would dearly liked to have found some relic of the old upright loom for I had been thrilled to read in the 'Burnt Njal' saga the dread-ful description of the Norns weaving the fate of men before the Battle of Clontarf. In the loom, the dangling weights were a row of human heads and the weft was woven of the entrails of men.

Flax was grown, spun and woven into linen. One of my early acquisitions at Iona was a sheaf of flax found in a peat bog where it had evidently been put to 'ret' (left for the softer parts to rot, leaving the fibres as lint to be spun into linen yarn). Old accounts and the contents of my mother's linen cupboard agree in show-ing how plentiful and fine supplies of linen were in the Highlands in the old days. Some of the yarn that was the evening task of the women of the household to spin, was sent to Musselburgh where the weaving of damask started, and woven into table-cloths.

Wool was either combed with special iron combs to remove the shorter fibres or 'noils', the resulting yarn being fine and hard and woven into a fabric like worsted, or else it was wound round the distaff like flax and the softer, coarser yarn used for woollen cloth. I always imagine that wool-cards for carding such wool were introduced about the same time as spinning-wheels. In the heady times of the Industrial Revolution the spinning of linen yarn, and to a lesser extent the weaving of linen, became an important rural industry in the central Highlands and Easter Ross and great efforts were made to encourage this and also the spinning of woollen yarn in some other parts of the Highlands. Spinning wheels were introduced and women were taught how to use them. On the west coast the kelp-burning boom was just starting and for a brief span of time there was occupation for all. Then, by a tragic twist of fate, the demand for hand-spinning of the early linen industry, which would have been such a boon to the women in the lean years that followed the collapse of the kelp boom, was killed by the introduction of cotton. Of course, the Highland women went on spinning wool for the domestic needs of their families and the spinning wheel gradually came into general use even in the Western Isles. When I was staying at Salen in Mull the last woman to use a spindle and distaff had just died and I was able to get them. They were only made of rough bits of wood, but the yarn rolled round the spindle was beautifully even in texture. I do not know when the combing of yarn was given up but I imagine that it was when people began to buy machine-made cloth about the same time as they bought cotton fabrics and gave up wearing linen ones. This would happen as easy means of communication spread through the Highlands and with it would go the weaving of tartan, which had been general.

The weaving of tartan raises the problem of dyeing. The colours mainly used in tartans are red, blue and green – the very ones that it is difficult to get from local dye plants. The great appreciation of colour by the people is proved by the immense trouble they must have taken to dye their fabrics in these colours. I did attempt some experiments in dyeing and by my dismal failures can appreciate the success of others. I never could have afforded or been able to obtain examples of the old very fine fabrics, but I did secure a number of home-spun blankets and bedcovers. Though warm, the blankets are very heavy and their owners were generally delighted to swap one of them for a modern blanket. Of all the things I collected I think that I got more satisfaction out of getting them than almost anything else. The bedcovers were generally covered with a bird's eye pattern and had deep borders at the ends. The blankets were white with a very large but thin over-check, often of two colours and with borders at the ends. One was of combed not carded yarn and was, I liked to think, a woman's plaid. It was the choice and blending of the colours that fascinated me. Very few were of brown, the easiest dye to get. Most of the blankets were checked with red and green, most often the red was the yellowish scarlet that one associates with costly madder. Indigo, also a favourite dye for women's skirts in some districts, was expensive and a troublesome one for the indigo had to be bought and the dyeing process involved soaking the wool in an ammonia solution. The ammonia used in the old days in the Highlands was urine, tactfully called 'home solution'. There was more diversity in the colouring of the bedcovers. Greys and purplish red were used as well as red and green. One was in red and yellow. Another pleasing fabric was drugget, used for women's skirts. The warp was of a neutral colour, often of grey, the weft was in alternate stripes of the same colour as the warp and of a brighter colour or two colours. I often felt that it was a pity that the weaving of drugget was not revived. Even in the making of rag rugs, both the shaggy ones with the ends loose or the tidy ones where the looped rags were pushed through the sacking, the women sometimes showed great taste and sense of colour.

In Strathdearn, when I was a child, the women still dyed with crotal, a coarse rock lichen that gives a good reddish brown. It needs no mordant, is easy to collect and the wool takes the dye readily. I have seen it being used in a huge pot over a fire outside. As always, the dye plant and the wool were arranged in alternate layers. In cases where a mordant is used it is sprinkled over the layer of dye plant. I was explaining the process to a visitor and she asked if tartan was made by arranging suitably thick layers of the different dye plants. In my youth I had ventured on a little dyeing myself in a pot borrowed from the kitchen. I was very delighted to obtain a wisp of brown wool, but the flavour of the lichen stuck to the pot. My parents thought they had been poisoned and I was not encouraged to proceed further. Years later, when the museum was at Laggan, Marjory Kendon, a professional handloom weaver, came to see it and paid many later visits. She was a kind friend for she taught me to spin with a spindle (I had taught myself to spin on my great-grandmother's wheel) and she set a warp upon a hand-loom I had required. She also taught me to recognise the bright yellowish shade of scarlet produced by madder. She had come to the Highlands on a quest to find the lichen (tartaricum) that soaked in ammonia gives a beautiful scarlet and she was able to collect some from rocks nearby. I gathered some of the lichen, used a bottle of Scrubbs ammonia and got a glorious colour, but failed to fix it and it dried out to a warm grey. I did not attempt this until after I had built the first of my cottages at Kingussie. It made a convenient and eminently suitable place for trying to carry on an ancient craft, but how unskilful I was compared to the women who had dyed the brilliant colours in my treasured bedcovers. I was more successful in getting a lovely pure yellow from the flowers of heather (ling). I had seen a coat and skirt dyed in this way while on Iona. The woman who had woven the stuff was dead but her friend told me what she had used. The greater part of a plant of heather only gives a yellowish brown, as do many others, especially bog myrtle (gale). One has to be very careful only to use the flowers in order to get the pure brilliant colour. I only made enough yarn for a stripe in a pair of gloves. I was told the skin of the roots was used. It took me a long time to fill a small pot with enough of this substance and it was a toilsome process for the rather poor red I got. In attempting vegetable dyeing, I very, very soon realised why the Highlanders used their colours in checks or stripes, generally narrow! When collecting, I used to ask about dye plants and was generally told that a luth mór (big plant) had been used, which did not make me much wiser, but once I was given a bit of lovely golden brown wool and I was told that it had been dyed by onion skins. I was delighted when a friend wanted enough yarn dyed with it to knit a cardigan because one was always glad to get orders for the women. Time passed and the yarn was not delivered. I went to expostulate and was told, 'We have had to eat an awful lot of onions'. Green, which was so much used in tartans, was made by mixing yellow which could be made from several plants, with blue for which there does not seem to be a native dye-plant and I was told that indigo was used. Apparently woad as well as madder will not grow in Scotland, which makes the Roman description of the Picts rather surprising. The chemicals such as alum that were used as mordents also had to be imported. I was once rather vaguely told that stag-horn moss could be used but I have never found any confirmation of this. A very old woman who visited the museum on Iona told me that her father had had a shop on Tiree and that she remembered as a child seeing bags of mordents and indigo. One can well understand that to wear clothes in colours that cost a good deal or took an immense amount of work to make would be a matter of prestige but I did wonder that the women of Barra and some of the other islands dyed their workaday skirts with indigo which had to be bought and was messy to dye, when crotal off the rocks would have given them a lovely brown dye at no expense and with very little trouble. I had the beautiful collection of vegetable dyes made for the Inverness Exhibition. Many visitors declared that they would try to do some dyeing themselves. I begged them to send me the results but I never received any so I doubt if any of them made a better job of vegetable dyeing than I did. It can however be done and a book has been published describing the success of one dyer.

To go back to the local craftsmen, as I have noted, in the Old Statistical Accounts one finds smiths, shoemakers, tailors and weavers but although I have read those of a good many parishes, I never came across the mention of a wood-worker. One realises that the joiners and carpenters who used steel tools to complete the new mason-built houses served wider areas and probably lived in the newly planned villages and belonged to a later stage of development and that nearly all the wooden vessels, the plunger churns, the cogs and the other staved vessels were probably made by them, although the craft of making 'feathered' staved vessels is certainly much older. One is then faced with the problem of what happened before that. A great many small wooden vessels were no doubt whittled out of a block of wood as anyone who is 'knacky' with his hands can do today. I have a theory that it would be easier to whittle a large square goblet than a round one. The Dunvegan Cup, the oldest wooden one we have, is of course of Irish origin but it was made at a time when the ways of Erin and the Highlands were closely linked and one poem about Finn MacCoul speaks of his angled cup. There had undoubtedly been staved vessels because some early Inverness silver quaichs are engraved with a design of feathered staves and I actually had a small finely made vessel of alternate staves of dark and light wood, the sides of which were joined together by feathering, which I was told was an ancient art practised by the tinkers.

The tinkers, whom it is now thought more polite to refer to as 'the travelling people', always told me that they were Romany (in other words Gypsies) but I think that they could claim a more interesting ancestry as being the descendants of the cairdean (cairds), the old travelling craftsmen of the Highlands who were in the days of oral tradition the recorders and preservers of the great Gaelic epics and poetry. Among their older skills were carving the handles of dirks in the traditional and interlaced patterns. They carried with them equipment for doing small-scale metal-work such as repairing or fashioning a brooch out of a silver coin. This craft survived in the doing of repairs to tin vessels. I read an old account of how one of them could tell the future by gazing into a drop of ink in the palm of the enquirer's hand and of course if you cross tinker women's hands with silver they will read the lines in your hand.

Another of the tinker's handicrafts was the making of horn spoons. The horn was boiled till it was soft and shaped by squeezing in a wooden mould. I had samples of both the spoons and the moulds and the tinkers used to bring their children to see these examples of their craft. I told them that if they would make some spoons I would sell them to visitors for them. They never did so, either because they had forgotten how to do so or because they thought that I would make an undue profit. They were most punctilious in always putting something in the collection box when they called. As they had access to people's back doors in carrying on their own small tradings, I thought that I might have been able to enlist their help as collectors, buying such old things as they could acquire, but it never came off. The only interesting thing that they sold me was an implement that they used in pearl fishing. It was a battered old tin cooking pot. The bottom had been replaced by a piece of glass held in place with candle grease. If it was pushed into the water so that the glass was below the surface the bed of the river could be more clearly seen and any freshwater mussels that might be there.

In the winter, tinkers make more permanent tents for themselves and, after I had moved the museum to Kingussie, I asked a tinker to set one up for me. He brought a bundle of long straight wands and a heap of old mackintoshes and other garments. Casually he stuck the ends of the wands into the ground in a perfect circle such as I could only have made by careful measurement with a peg and bit of string. Then he tied the tops together and arranged over them the pile of old clothes. Inside, on the bare ground, he made a little hearth of flat stones and beside it stuck a stick with a hooked end into the ground and on it hung a kettle. Beside it he made up a bed with no mattress but with a number of blankets and sheets. Every party of tinkers who came to the museum used to say they could have made a much better one.

15

Craftsmen's Tools
and Household Plenishings

WITH the making of the roads, the pacification of the country and the agricultural reforms there were great changes in the outward circumstances of the people and one might say that the Steel and Cast Iron Age set in. The new lay-out of the farms was accompanied by the use of the improved plough and by the introduction of other, more sophisticated and imported implements. I am not sure if there is a definite date when the use of the scythe instead of the sickle transformed harvesting. The change was evidently sporadic. It was certainly later than the plough or the introduction of field-drainage. Of course, the tools that one saw in use, such as saws and hammers, became available to everyone but the factor that was most evident was a new way of house-building and of making household furnishings and was due to the coming of a new kind of craftsmen. The second half of the eighteenth century was a great age for the building of bridges and the re-building of churches in the Highlands, which involved the employment of masons. The fashion of building stone-and-lime houses spread among the gentry and then to farmers and involved the employment of masons, joiners and carpenters and to accommodate these tradesmen villages were founded or enlarged. Sir James Grant of Grant was particularly active in founding such villages but there was a healthy rivalry among some of the great landlords in doing this. The line of villages along the Spey, of which Kingussie is one, is an example. The textile industries were booming, the power-loom had not come into use and the number of hand-loom weavers increased. There were also more fishermen in the newly stimulated fishing industry who were also accommodated in newly founded villages.

Man's mastery over the forests reached a new phase with the use of steel tools. Of course, in the Lowlands this stage had long been reached. It was not till the later eighteenth century that it became general in the Highlands. In the great lumbering industry of Strathspey, the logs were floated down the river to the sea at Garmouth. This was the easiest form of transport and one still sees logs being floated from the remoter forests of Norway but the Highlands, especially, the eastern Highlands, soon learnt to use small-scale water mills to turn the abundant supply of local water power to good account sawing logs. The supply of suitable wood gradually changed the interior of the rooms. Floorboards, window frames and plastered ceilings came into more and more general use. A typical example was the box-bed enclosed by shutters of planking. People have told me that in the eighteenth century it was the accepted furnishing of the kitchen and parlour as well as the bedrooms in the upland farmhouses. When I was collecting, I saw several surviving specimens of one.

The new style of room required a new style of furnishing. This also spread downwards to lower social levels. As means of transport improved, more and more good furniture, made by the craftsmen of Edinburgh or Perth, was imported and it was copied by the local craftsmen. I was always delighted when I came across examples of their work because it exemplified the diversity and yet the close association of the old Highland society. I think that kists, which by the eighteenth century were regarded as necessary possessions, had been to some extent in use in earlier times, but tables and cupboards, most convenient articles of furniture, now came into general use. A characteristic piece of furniture was the séiseach, a word often anglicised into 'sofa'. It was a long wooden bench with a back and arms at the ends. There may have been earlier examples but all those that I saw were of this period and they illustrated how dependent the people were upon availability of supplies and material. I had a beauty from Strathspey. It was made of splendid pine wood with dark grainings. The back was formed of a number of upright bars turned on a lathe. Other examples from elsewhere were made of less and less wood and less and less good quality, down to a specimen with merely one bar along the back.

To complete the furnishings of the best parlour of my youth, there were always rag rugs, some of them with skilfully blended colours. In even the poorer homes, windows were discreetly veiled by stiffly starched, machine-made lace curtains. All their plenishings were imported and not particularly characteristic but I noticed two things that were. One was that almost always in the best room there was a little table or a small kist with a cloth over it and arranged upon it a few little old treasures such as a finely made horn toddy-ladle, a snuff mull or some small treasure brought from overseas. The other thing that I remember is the welcome that I so often received, gracious as well as warm, the heritage of an old and very proud civilisation. That is a thing a poor folk museum can only exhibit by the manners of the attendants who show people around. Did I always thus exhibit this admirable characteristic of my race – I am afraid the answer is 'No'!

The metal utensils of the houses also underwent a great change during the second half of the eighteenth century. Tin came into use for a number of things and supplied a new trade to the tinkers in mending them. Iron vessels raise rather a problem in my mind. Undoubtedly, iron cooking pots hanging over the fire on a chain from the roof were ancient and traditional equipment of a Highland house although I have been told that it was possible to boil things in a skin bag hanging well above the fire if there was plenty of water in it. To shape iron pots simply by hammering would, one imagines, be a difficult task and so it is no wonder that they are scarce. I only managed to obtain one specimen. Of course, in the old days of great scarcity of iron, worn-out pots would have been made into something else – for instance I had in the collection what was obviously a bit of a dirk that was made into a contraption for weighing. With improved communications and the mass-production of cast iron objects at Carron and other iron mills, cooking pots for hanging over the fire and made of cast iron became very plentiful even in the poorer districts of the Highlands, and I was able to get many surviving specimens. They were of all sizes including a very large one that was evidently for dyeing – I was lucky enough to see one being used for this purpose – but a young visitor to the museum thought that it must have been a chief's porridge pot.

I think that the large flat pots with covers must have come in fairly late because they were made of so much iron and their transport would be difficult. They were used for baking bread (as late as the 1780s flour was a luxury in most parts of the Highlands) or for cooking meat and the fire was built up all round and on top of them. I met people who had actually eaten food cooked in them and they said that it tasted specially good. I asked how the woman who was doing the cooking managed to know when the food was ready and was told that she had to calculate and that, enclosed in such a pot, food was not easily over-cooked. I stupidly did not ask where the cooking was done, for such a pot, if covered with burning peat, would not have fitted into the fireplace under a 'hanging chimney' of the more sophisticated type of local building but must have been used when the hearth was on the floor in the middle of the house. As a matter of fact bread and meat were luxuries only partaken of on festive occasions and the cooking was probably done outside for the benefit of the large community that shared in wedding festivities. The ancient spirit of neighbourliness and hospitality lingered though the cooking pot might be modern.

16
Lighting

M EANS of lighting varied in different districts according to what materials were available. About the time that I started to collect there was rather a vogue among antique dealers for 'Peermen' (from the north-east Scots for 'poor man'). It was an iron stand with a clip at the top for holding a splinter of wood and the term arose because the usual means of lighting was by a lighted splinter of wood, generally held by a child, but if a beggar asked for a night's lodging he was expected to hold the burning splinter which, as it was generally made of the resinous wood of a pine tree, was called a 'fir candle'.

In the Highlands iron for making such stands was too precious to be used in this way. It was as a rarity that I did hear of one from Strathnairn being put up for auction, but the bidding ran too high for me. The Highlanders, however, had an economical substitute – a stone with a hole in it into which a stick was stuck and an iron clip to hold the fir candle was fixed into the top. As it stood by the fire and became black with peat soot it was called the gille dubh – 'black boy'. But such things would be unlikely to survive. I had one but the stick was obviously new. I did come across individual clips which could have been used for such a stand or for fitting between the stones of a wall and I was told that fir candles were often carefully arranged to dry upon one of the open-work girdles characteristic of Strathspey and Atholl and may well have been lighted, but in the actual accounts I have read, they were either held or placed upon a stone. To us it seems to be a meagre way of lighting a room.

The other way of lighting was by the 'cruisies'. These are generally thought to be something particularly Highland but, as a matter of fact, their use was mainly confined to districts where wood was scarce, as is the case in many of the western Islands, or to fishing settlements, because fish oil was generally burnt in them, though mutton fat could be used. I did not attempt to make a census of cruisies and, as far as I know, a study of their distribution has not been made, but it would be quite interesting to know the exact facts. The wicks were made of the pith of a rush which it was the children's job to peel, leaving a narrow strip of the outside to keep the pith from breaking. Cruisies themselves were made locally. Blacksmith's anvils sometimes had hollows into which the smith could hammer and shape the thin sheet of iron and, from Tiree, the museum received the gift of a stone with two hollows that had been used for that purpose. Considering how economical the people were in their use of iron, I always feel surprised that they did not make their lamps of something else – for instance, from a hollowed stone or from clay, especially the latter, for clay can be found in many parts of the Highlands.

I have never seen a cruisie in use but I have spoken to many people who can remember seeing them in byres and barns. One of these reminiscences gave me one of the greatest thrills that I had in showing people round the museum. I told of it in a book that I wrote, *Highland Folk Ways*, but I look back on it with so much pleasure that I must allude to it in the course of my memories. A party of youngish people accompanied by one little old lady came to see the museum. The young ones were chatty and quite ignorant of the old country ways. The little old lady was shy and silent. I answered their questions. She said nothing. In due course, we came to the collection of various things for giving light and suddenly the little old lady exclaimed, 'A cruisgean!' Colour came into her face, her voice rose above a whisper. She described how she had gone with friends to the barn where some lads were threshing. Two cruisies were blazing and against their light the arms of the young men went up and down as they threshed and it glistened on the beads of sweat. Then the animation faded from her face and her voice dropped as she said that the youths were gone and so had all the party of friends and the barn itself was an old unused ruin and yet that the sight of the cruisie had brought it all back to her.

I rather imagine that hinged brackets for fir candles may first have been used in castle halls and then in the houses and later in the steadings of the lesser gentry. Torches may have really figured upon greater occasions. When staying at Dunvegan it was splendid to hear Dame Flora MacLeod of MacLeod tell of a forebear who had been visiting in the south and had been taunted that at home he had not a fine candelabra like that of his vainglorious host. He wagered that he had, and when the visit was returned, one night he took his guest to MacLeod's Tables (the flat hills one sees from the castle windows) and there served him dinner surrounded by fully-armed clansmen bearing flaming torches. He won his bet. A similar tale is told of another chief. They may be apocryphal but they illustrate the old political organisation of the Highlands with the supreme importance of manpower.

By the eighteenth century, if not earlier, fir candles and cruisies were going down the social scale and were moving from the reception rooms of the house to the lesser offices. The Highland gentry came more and more into contact with people from the south and came to adopt their customs, especially for entertaining. They began to use fashionable furniture (or local copies of it) and table equipment, and as they certainly had candlesticks, so they must have used candles. These were made of mutton fat at first by dipping a string into a pot of boiling fat. I never heard of beeswax being used and, before the introduction of improved agriculture and of large-scale sheep-farming, they must have been rather a strain upon the laird's or tacksman's resources to produce. With the introduction of hardy sheep, not only by the great flock-masters but by the upland hill-farmers, mutton fat must have been more easily come by and goods from the south being more and more available, tin candle moulds were introduced and candles were made by threading a wick through them and then pouring in the fat. Several people have told me that older relations told them when they were children it was a treat and an honour to hold the end of the wick while the fat was poured in. Tin lasts well and I had a good many candle moulds and could have got more. They were generally made in groups of six but there were also single ones, which suggests that for many people candles were still a luxury.

When, as a very old woman, I tell people that I can remember when, although the sitting room was lamp-lit, bedroom candle-sticks were put out in the hall to light each member of the family to bed, they think how primitive we were. It is salutary to remember that there were times long before, when a candle, and before that a lighted cruisie or a splinter of burning wood, was all the light that there was. Yet people led full and busy lives in what we look back on as 'the good old days'.

I really appreciated my own folk museum because I had a modicum of knowledge and appreciation of history, customs and arts of the past. By written matter pinned on the walls I tried very hard to convey to visitors something of the background of the things that they were looking at. It is the homely, humble things of life that best can illustrate how little outward material circumstances can make or mar human potential.

17

Transport

IN these random recollections I lean rather heavily on travel-ling about. Although the Highlands and Islands comprises only a small geographical area, there is a great diversity of ter-rain and social development within it, so that the lie of the land and its dispersion in the ocean do not tend to easy travelling. I have however a much more fundamental reason for dwelling upon means of transport in the Highlands. Means of access indeed have played a decisive part in the area's social and economic devel-opment, or alas, viewed from certain angles, in its deterioration.

Although, before the road-making of the eighteenth century, the people of the Highlands were also hampered in making contacts outside by their language and very different mode of life, they were remarkably mobile within the Highlands. Cattle raiding was so extensive that a recognised custom arose of the giving of the 'Raider's Collop', *ie* a small share of the booty to the owner of any land through which the raiders made their way. It is also important to remember how mobile the individual High-landers were by boat as well as upon foot. As a matter of course they walked huge distances. One remembers best traditions of distances they were accustomed to walk in areas where, al-though one now travels by very different means of transport, one can appreciate how very long the road can be. For instance, Mac-kintosh of Mackintosh, whose home was at Moy close to Tomatin, employed 'running footmen' who would take a letter from Moy in the valley of the Findhorn, across the valley of the Spey and over the Cairngorms to a friend in Deeside, and return with an answer all in the space of 24 hours, at a time when the rivers were unbridged and such roads as there were, were mere tracks. Much later in the eighteenth century, the women in Strathdearn still carried their wares to market in Inverness on foot and returned in the evening, if they lived far up the glen. This would entail a walk of over twenty miles each way.

The development of the roads is a greater and more valuable subject for study and effective illustration than the railways, because of its historical, social and economic importance. The story in every district, parish or glen varied. Roughly speaking, in the Highlands there were a number of recognised tracks but exceedingly few roads and those very bad, being maintained by 'statute labour' – work imposed upon the people who occupied the land adjoining the roads. The military roads constructed by General Wade in the 1720s and early 1730s were a landmark, but it was only gradually they were improved and added to in order to make them really useful for civilian purposes. Another roadmaking landmark was the Highland Roads and Bridges Act of 1803, setting up a Parliamentary Commission and providing special funds for their extension, improvement and upkeep. When the railways came, the roads' importance was diminished in the distribution system, but the coming of the motor car, which came into general use just before the First World War, has once again established their supremacy. The immediate effect of their reconstruction, involving a great deal of labour, was to bring in a large number of temporary workers and to give some employment to local people, but this activity was ephemeral and ended with the completion of the work. I have actually seen how, in the remaking of the A9, mechanisation reduced even this temporary influx of work. Extensive improvements carried out during the 1920s were made by a gang of navvies. The more drastic remaking at present being completed was mainly done by machines operated by a few skilled mechanics.

I have seen many changes in the means of transport since I started collecting for the museum, but my personal memory goes much further back to days before the motor car, to narrow roads with high cambers that got very dusty in the summer but were safe and pleasant to walk, ride or bicycle along, to travelling in a horse-drawn mail gig and charabanc, to being driven to a party in one's best hat on a wet day in an open pony cart, to the majestic approach of a Puffing Billy at harvest time and the shame when one's pony turned tail. By the time I had a folk museum to collect for I had a motor car – not quite a museum specimen – but many of the roads I drove along were still in a primitive state. I am glad I can remember the drive from Glencoe by the old road. The surface had got a bit out of repair and it slanted steeply up a slope that, especially when one had to reverse at the hairpin bends, looked almost sheer. There was not another soul upon the road. The engine of the car had become rather heated. I stopped and looked back down the glen. The massacre of Glencoe is one of the best known episodes in Highland history. One pictured the homesteads of the hospitable, unsuspecting clansmen beside the windings of the river Coe, darkness blotting out the doings of that shameful night and the plight of the fleeing survivors, in cold and storm, over the steep hillside upon the other side of the glen. Remembrance of its tragic past heightened my appreciation of the beauty of the place. It happened to be at that time when a belated spring rushes into summer. I had stayed at Onich and had taken the ferry across Loch Leven, the bridge having not yet been built. Along the pleasant coastal land there was a tinge of green upon the woodlands and the flowers that grow there were in full bloom before the foliage of the trees should hide them from view. Better still the lovely spring grass was growing strongly and the ewes could feed their lambs and were contented and so were the lesser nursing mothers, the rabbits with their prolific families, and the little brown voles that make their careful stores in the tussocks. But at the point that I had reached, high up the pass, the grass looked dun and sapless and had not stirred from its long quiescence during the prolonged winter of the Highland uplands. From the Glen with its stories and its contrasts one's eyes travelled to the higher hills. Their shaggy hides of heather had, I knew, their darker winter colours but, seen through miles of sun-lit air, they took on a new look and seemed to be at the threshold of the Infinite. King David, the psalmist, must have seen the same look when he raised his eyes to the so different hills of Palestine. Since that drive, I have several times travelled with speed and comfort through Glencoe by the new road, but I could not have stopped the car in the middle of the road to get out and look at the view and if I had I would not have seen it just that way.

Ferries, where they still exist and have not been replaced by bridges, have changed a lot in my days. Even the ferry to Skye, from Kyle of Lochalsh to Kyleakin, was very primitive. A pier of rough construction – the gaps between the stones were so wide that I am not sure if cement was used at all – was so low that at high tide part of it was submerged and at low tide it was covered with slippery sea-slime. The boat was an open one with a platform upon it to accommodate, I forget if, at first, it was one or two cars. If the tide was out, one had to drive down to the slippery end of the pier, manoeuvre the car round and drive along two planks onto this platform. The crew then obligingly arranged wooden blocks to prevent the car from running off the platform into the sea. One day there was a stiffish breeze blowing contrary to the tide-race and the strait was worked up into choppy waves. There had been some debate among the crew whether they would cross before I embarked and they continued to argue whether they would do so. I had had an early breakfast and started to eat some sandwiches that I had brought with me. I offered some to a man and woman who were also crossing. The woman took one and I heard the man mutter what sounded like, 'What call have you to be doing what you are, at what may be the last hour of your life?' She desisted. I went on munching. I doubted if my last hour was approaching, but I was quite certain that I would not enjoy eating those sandwiches when we got to the rough water in the middle of the Kyle.

Mr and Mrs Seton Gordon had kindly asked me to stay with them. He is best known for his writings on the Cairngorms and its eagles but he and his wife lived at Duntulm in Trotternish on the western coast of Skye. If the day was clear, one could see part of the Outer Hebrides as a long line on the horizon. Generally it was only a grey outline but if the sunlight caught it at a certain angle it glowed, a magical land – a veritable Tir nan Òg.

Mrs Seton Gordon had friends all round her. Before my coming, she had done some prospecting and told me that one woman had an old wooden bowl and she had arranged for us to go and see it. She would also speak about a job she had found for the daughter. We duly visited the woman and found her in a state of acute embarrassment. The daughter had said people would be laughing at them for keeping such an old-fashioned thing about the place and had taken it away. She was sent for and the pretty little minx had evidently thought that it was all a joke. She said rather airily that she could not rightly say if she could find the bowl to bring it back. Her face fell as Mrs Gordon said she could not recommend a girl who unkindly destroyed something other people valued and had come specially to see. Almost weeping, the girl said she would try to get the bowl back and slipped from the room. We valiantly made conversation with the mother during a long pause. Then she reappeared with the bowl. It was still wet from a recent washing but a faint aroma of the place to which she had consigned it still clung to it.

I am ignorant of the history of the coming of the steamers, the mail and passenger services round the Islands, McCallum Orme & Company, the old cargo line upon which I had made a most informative trip (seeing cargoes being loaded and unloaded is more interesting than reading tables of statistics) and the 'puffers' that brought coal to the Islands, so amusingly portrayed in Neil Munro's *Para Handy* tales and such a nuisance to me when my little attempt at a garden upon Iona was periodically ruined by the carts coming to collect the coal.

The air service to the Long Island started about the same time as I bought the church upon Iona and I did my trips to the Islands by steamer. I travelled at the more clement seasons of the year and on the whole the Minch was kind to me. My most vivid recollection from such trips was once, when the steamer to Barra was very late, I saw the walls of Kisimul Castle rising straight from their rocky base in the sea and looming palely in the moonlight. It was the perfect setting for the ideal romantic tale – such as the love-story of Mary, the heiress to MacLeod of Dunvegan, with MacNeil of Barra, but it had an unhappy ending and Mary was married off to a Campbell. There was, however, a tradition that after Campbell's death, the two were reunited. In a more successful operation, MacNeil and his men barred the castle gate against a King's Messenger with his escort, who had been charged to deliver a warrant. They tossed down rocks which nearly brained the intruders, who retreated leaving the warrant upon the ground. As the lights of the steamer passed close to the castle on the way into Castlebay, their faint golden reflection tinged the white moonlight. The effect was most eerie. The harbour lights were, however, blotting out the fainter radiance on the castle walls. They recalled my thought to the very present problem of whether the hotel would still be open. It was. The belated guest was welcomed and fed. The hotel keepers of the Islands were always obliging and helpful however late or early one arrived or departed. The attitude of some mainland hoteliers if one were travelling in the winter was sometimes rather less than gracious!

I do not know how much the increased travel by air has affected the Islanders' attitude to the coming and going of the steamers. At almost any hour when the ship approached the quay one would see a group of people awaiting her arrival. Visitors were to be seen off or welcomed. People on the shore snatched a few moments chat with their friends on board and some passengers hurried ashore for the same purpose. When it was time for the ship to leave, people began to hurry up and down the gangway. Sometimes there was a delay and the captain rang a warning bell. There were scurryings and much quiet amusement among the spectators before the gangway was hauled away and ropes cast off from the bollards. Pleasant memories linger.

It always amused me to think how completely the attitude of many of the island women justified Darwin's theory that acquired characteristics cannot be inherited. In my young days one would have said that there must have been a lot of Viking blood in these women's veins. Nowadays one would use a more scientific jargon about the transmission of genes. During the intervening centuries the fabric of island life largely depended upon the use of boats – birlinns, fishing boats and steamers – and yet among the women it seemed to be rather the done thing to expect to be seasick if the sea was not as calm as a mill pond. Friends, who have happened to be travelling to the Islands at the time the girls were returning from herring gutting in the south eastern ports, have spoken of the joy of hearing the ship being filled by the sound of the girls' singing, but if the sea was in the least rough, the melody quickly died away.

When we planned the Exhibition at Inverness we arranged for a section to illustrate the development of the local railway system. Maps and diagrams of the development of the Highland Railway illustrated a story full of interest. As part of an upsurge of national enterprise, the railway boom brought lines run by the great companies as far as Perth and Aberdeen by the middle of the nineteenth century. But it was by the initiative of local men that a line from Inverness through Forres was built and then linked at Keith to a line from Aberdeen owned by the Great North of Scotland Railway Co. A yet more ambitious project by Joseph Mitchell – the Highland Superintendent of Roads – was the making in the early 1860s of a line from Dunkeld just north of Perth, over Drumochter and down Strathspey to join the existing line at Forres. This signalled the birth of the Highland Railway. The construction of the direct branch from Aviemore to Inverness came later, in the 1890s.

The old Highland Railway held a place in the pride and affection of the local people that, of course, has been lost now that the railways have been nationalised. I feel that I am blameworthy in not having secured some characteristic mementoes of it. Unfortunately, shortage of cash, space, encouragement and time forced me to use what I had upon more obvious things. The stories of the lines to the north, to Oban and Mallaig (made with the great innovation of the use of concrete) and to Kyle of Lochalsh, must all be full of points of local interest.

The vast importance of changes in the means of transport is mainly a negative one, apart from the very mixed fortunes of the fisheries and the tourist industry which, although it has increased in volume, has not I think, advanced in value to the local community. One could not indicate in a museum that the old fashion of a family with a staff renting a house for the season, or of individuals staying in hotels for some periods, brought in more money than hitch-hikers or caravanners who bring their own supplies besides being a nuisance upon the roads, but it ought to be studied and brought to the notice of those authorities who are responsible. What I think could be shown or somehow be indicated are the changes that improved means of communication have made to the way of life in the Highlands. Of course, exceptions abounded – I myself have seen a cottage with a hearth on the floor in the middle of the building – but on the whole, and speaking generally, I would like to suggest that in the more accessible parts of the mainland and in the more advanced islands, the coming of the roads stimulated many other changes and marks a period in local social history. With a change from the hearth upon the ground in the middle of the main room of the cottage would come a development not only in the amenities of life but also in its individuality. The wearing of the kilt would diminish. Home-spun and hand-woven woollen and lined cloth would be replaced by boughten woollen and cotton cloth. So far as I know no-one has studied when, actually, the hanging chimney was invented, but I would suggest that, as with the abolition of the great hall and the custom of eating in family, privacy became usual among those who had lived in castles about the end of the seventeenth century, and the fashion spread downwards among the lesser gentry, many of whom still lived in houses of the traditional style. This would involve a partition wall and a hanging chimney. In the closely integrated society of the Highlands, and according to all indications, the new arrangement spread and with it would come the introduction of a good many of the plenishings that we now think typical of a Highland cottage such as the swee and the séiseach. When I got to Kingussie and was able to build cottages, I illustrated this great change in the interiors of Highland cottages. The Lewis Cottage had a hearth on the ground in the middle of the living part of the cottage. The Inverness-shire Cottage – most unfortunately burnt down – had a hanging chimney. I think that it is essential for a folk museum to illustrate this important change in the arrangement of the interior of the buildings because, with it, was going on an alteration in the people's main source of livelihood. The most important feature of their lives which one would be hard put to indicate in a museum is that they were ceasing to be subsistence farmers dependent for their actual food upon a severe and unpredictable climate. The new growing dependence upon distant markets bears especially hard upon many of the very areas that the crofting legislation and organisation try to maintain under an outdated agricultural system. The people had not only ceased to be subsistence farmers but were gradually ceasing to depend upon their own handiwork or that of local craftsmen for their clothes and belongings. The coming of the railways hastened the process but unfortunately the useful railways and steamers were only the ultimate finger tips of greater lines of communication, which were beginning to saturate our food supplies with imports from overseas. The constant dread of hunger had thinned the population of the glens in the days of subsistence farming. Now the fact that it did not pay to cultivate most of the land emptied them yet further.

18

The Social Pattern

IN trying to preserve the relics of the past of one's people it is essential to realise what that past was like that created the social setting from which the relics came. I very much deplore that in the preponderant part of the work done on social life in the Highlands the historical background has been ignored and attention has been almost entirely focused upon one limited and atypical part of the Highlands.

My remembrance of a visit to Frilandsmuseet, the large folk museum near Copenhagen, is that of rows of exactly-spaced-out little houses, each on an identically-sized plot of land, each one discreetly veiled from its neighbours by bushes and small trees and each one approached by a neat gravelled path. These specimens of the local cottage building styles of Denmark made me think of the bottles of fish in neatly arranged rows in the South Kensington Natural History Museum that as a child I used to hurry through. The academically minded would derive great benefit from studying these specimens but they were woefully unlike the lovely darting silvery creatures that I so often watched and alas so often failed to catch. I am very ignorant about Denmark but, judging from two very pleasant drives I was taken through the country, I am pretty sure that this folk museum gives a very distorted impression of rural life there, past or present.

At Skansen, very skilful – a modern writer would say 'imaginative' – use was made of the undulation of the ground. The little houses were scattered and there were no straight gravelled paths, so the effect was more natural. Even so, although I was never lucky enough to set foot outside Stockholm itself, I do not imagine that this peasant community represents the country life of so sophisticated and prosperous a country as Sweden. Lille-hammer in Norway made a very different impression upon me. Up a glen, the homes of people of a different status – profes-sional, largish farming, small-holding and fishermen – were built upon the varying types of land that were appropriate to them. One's own country background enabled one to appreciate the rightness of the placing. The God-given gift of artistic creation had enabled the founder to convey the sense of a living commu-nity of the past. By a strange paradox, the artificially organised crofting areas of a large part of the Western Isles and mainland of the Highlands in some respects resemble the artificial lay-out of Frilandsmuseet – of course, omitting the neat little gravelled paths – while at the same time as economically, they are an artifi-cially retarded agricultural development, the crofting areas contain the best hunting ground for would-be makers of folk museums.

I have already written something about the great changes in the appearance of the Highland countryside, both in the east and the west. In the latter, the crofting legislation of the 1880s added security of tenure to the new lay-out of the countryside intro-duced in the early years of last century – that of similarly sized smallholdings theoretically sufficient to maintain the occupiers. Subsidiary sources of income were derived from a declining fishing industry, employment upon public work such as road repairing and in tweed weaving organised as a cottage industry, somewhat on the lines of the Scots linen industry of the eighteenth century or the medieval English woollen industry. I have never heard that any attempt was made to specialise upon an individual holding. Apart from rather widely dispersed minis-ters, priests, teachers and doctors and a few general merchants, the inhabitants were all of the same class and occupation, that of crofting. Within the past half century this monotony has been slightly varied, because the regulations have been changed to allow crofters to acquire more land and, as is very obvious to the eye, an increasing number of crofts have been allowed to go out of cultivation. At the same time, partly because of the remoteness of their situation, the old tongue of the Highlands, the Gaelic, has survived as the current language and, certainly down to the twentieth century in those districts where the locally dominant form of religion did not discourage them, some of the old stories and traditions also survived. Lack of access to markets as well as lack of means accounted for the retention of primitive goods and chattels. A more fundamental inheritance is the prevailing good breeding and gentle manners of the people (until they are exposed to the effects of tourism). These have been handed down from the old social organisation of the Highlands, which was highly complex and aristocratic in origin. I feel very strongly that this is not sufficiently understood or taken into account in specialised studies of individual aspects of Highland culture or of modern local conditions.

It is often forgotten that in old Scots law there were layers of entitlement to the possession of land. The whole of Scotland belonged to the king. He delegated the superiorities of large slices of it to favoured individuals – according to the practice in feudal times – in return for military and administrative services. Such land was of course already occupied and the gift of superiority merely inserted another subject between the occupiers and the sovereign. In certain areas of the Highlands, forfeiture resulted in a more powerful and adroit chief upon the right side of the law obtaining possession of a district already organised as part of the lands of another chief. Andrew McKerral's *Kintyre in the Seventeenth Century* gives an illuminating analysis of what happened in one such case and of course I had read with special interest about the similar fate of Islay, Lewis, Mull and Iona itself. By feus, wadsets (a form of mortgage), leases and, although undefined by law, the old right of 'kindly tenancy', the rights to occupy land in the Highlands in general were filtered down in successive layers. Bonds of maintenance and of service made further complexities. The size of the clan, the nature of the tenures by which the clansmen held their land and the boundaries of the areas that they occupied were infinitely varied and were subject to change and modification. Only one fact stands out immutably. The Highlands were not a single-class peasant community.

Clans originally developed as a result of the failure of central government to maintain law and order in the Highlands. When virtually the 'Law of the Jungle' prevailed, 'a man's hand had to keep his head', and he had to depend upon the support of his neighbours. The form of association that developed was unique to the Highlands. It evolved and was not statutorily created and was therefore so varied that only the broadest generalisations about it can be attempted.

Clann is the Gaelic for 'children'. In theory, and also to a large extent in fact, the clansmen were the direct descendants of the eponym of the clan – the individual who by high birth and a rich inheritance, as for instance in the case of the Macdonalds descended from Donald, the grandson of Somerled, or by skill and good fortune as in the case of the Mackenzies from Kenneth of Kintail, had been able to establish a family. The founder's descendants had families which in turn had families of their own, all claiming relationship with each other. We do not think of the ties of relationship beyond second cousins. In a couple of centuries the chief of a clan would have hundreds of cousins, some of them sixth or seventh ones.

The structure of the clan, however, was not egalitarian. The eldest son of the chief succeeded to the estate and other sons were provided for within it, generally with the security of a house, and they provided for their younger sons within their share. The structure of chief and heads of cadet branches with many grades below them was usual, binding the clan together on the loyalty of the clansmen to the chief. This of course is proverbial. What title as existed to the land – Crown charter or feu – was in the chief's name. He was their intermediary with the authorities, their leader in battle, the administrator of justice – or in his name these duties were delegated to the heads of the cadet branches. His hospitality was ever open to his clansmen. His piper played for them. MacLeod of MacLeod employed three pipers and a fiddler. Events in his family such as the birth of the heir or the marriage of a daughter, and above all the pomp and display of his own funeral, were their social occasions. Such a society was the perfect setting for the epics, poetry and music of the clarsach of ancient Gaeldom.

The clans varied very much in size and fortune. The rapid growth of the Campbells, followed by that of the Mackenzies, was at the expense of many others. Some chiefs had Crown charters for their land, others only feus that involved the obligation of military service. Many of them held scattered portions of land. Occasionally the lands of two clans were intermixed. Some chiefs had no land at all and their clans lived as a client upon the land of a more powerful host. The relationship of the MacRaes with the Mackenzies was an especially happy one. Inevitably there were areas where the aggrandisement of one clan destroyed the social organisation of its previous owners. It is particularly unfortunate that the Campbells of Shawfield should have acquired Islay, the ancient centre of the Lordship of the Isles.

As the clans were mainly developed as a means of protection and there was a strong military element in their organisation, the natural increase among the clansmen was welcome, although by the eighteenth century the population of the limited areas of arable land in the Highlands had become heavy. This was unfortunate because it was difficult for the people to go elsewhere. It was exceptional to join another clan. The relative poverty of the Highlanders and the difference in language, dress and the ways of life, besides a mutual antipathy, made it difficult for them to settle outside the Highlands before the later eighteenth century.

By way of illustrating the kind of evolution which individual clans could show, I may mention in particular the Grants and the Mackintoshes. Both my father's and my mother's families came from the eastern Highlands. I am a deplorably bad genealogist compared to the elders and betters of my childhood, but fortunately my family background is well documented. From many of the details of the social structure in Strathdearn and Strathspey and surrounding districts, from Highland friends and relations and from later studies I know that, with infinite local variations, there were very complex social patterns all over the Highlands. And the bits that I know most about are also well documented by the gigantic hoard of Seafield Papers; by Sir William Fraser's *Chiefs of Grant*; and A M Mackintosh's *The Mackintoshes and Clan Chattan*. Also, on the more social side, Mrs Anne Grant of Laggan's *Letters from the Mountains* and Elizabeth Grant's *Memoirs of a Highland Lady*, and, on a more down-to-earth level, by my own forebear's farming account book.

In Strathspey in the middle of the fifteenth century, the head of the family, Sir Duncan Grant, having married the heiress to Freuchie and other lands in Strathspey, he and his successors acquired the many fragments of land held by the different tenures into which Strathspey had been divided. Eventually the consolidated territory – the land between the two Craigellachies – was erected into a regality, the form of Scots land tenure that delegated to the holder most completely all legal and administrative rights. In the course of this consolidation the 'Clan of Grant' is first mentioned. Three fortunate chiefs obtained lands outwith this solid chunk of Grant territory and these they bestowed upon younger sons on a heritable tenure but, on the whole, younger sons and other leading men were provided with wadsets, and leases. They in turn had to provide by further subdivision for younger ones. There is at the same time very clear evidence that individuals already occupying some of the land adopted the surname of Grant and held land, and as it was usual in the Highlands to use patronymics this would have been a simple matter. Strathspey, however, as we learn from the parish registers, was never solely inhabited by Grants.

It is necessary to remember that the infinite number of gradations of clansmen also existed in clans where chiefs had not such compact estates as had Grant of Grant. The story of Clan Mackintosh is more eventful and complex than that of Clan Grant. It is difficult to summarise the account of the land that the chief held because the situation underwent many changes. The founder of the family, Shaw Mac-an-Tòisich (Mackintosh – son of a thane), was, according to the generally accepted clan tradition, a younger son of the ancient (Macduff) Earls of Fife, and was in the army with which Malcolm IV subdued the rebellious province of Moray in 1163. He was given a grant which may have only been verbal, for no written copy of it exists, of Petty and Breachly in the fertile Laich of Moray and the Forest of Strathdearn in the upper Valley of the Findhorn. In spite of many vicissitudes of fortune, his family acquired a great deal more land but it was in scattered portions mainly in Strathnairn, Strathdearn and Badenoch and they lost some as they gained more. It was ironical that for centuries the only Crown charter that they had was for land in Lochaber that they vainly and constantly tried, sometimes by force of arms, to get possession of. As the chiefs changed their style of address in their signatures to documents, 'of Connage' (in the Laich of Moray), 'of Tordarroch' (in Strathnairn), 'of Dunachton' (in Badenoch), *etc*, they apparently moved their principle residence, but about 1700 a new house was built at Moy, in Strathdearn, on some of the land originally granted to them, and this became their headquarters. In spite of territorial insecurities Bishop Leslie, writing in the time of Mary, Queen of Scots, cited the Mackintoshes as an example of the devotion of clansmen to their chief. Many of these clansmen were resident upon land that was not actually owned by Mackintosh and which was also occupied by members of other clans. The list of officers in the regiment raised by the wife of the chief in the '45 is an interesting illustration of this. Another great source of strength for Mackintosh was the support given by other members of Clan Chattan (a federation of clans and families that is, I think, unique in Highland history) and especially by Macbeans, Macgillivrays and MacQueens. The leases and feus held by families of these clans make a complicated pattern of occupation in Strathnairn, Strathdearn and Badenoch.

If one has occasion to scrutinise other districts in the Highlands it is not uncommon to find a far from simple pattern of occupation by different families at different levels – as, for instance, the Robertsons (Clan Donnachaidh) and branches of the Stewarts in Atholl, which the Earl of Atholl (a member of the Murray family) held of the king, or on the lands of Macleod of Macleod where among a great variety of families holding land, some were believed to be descendants of the ancient inhabitants, such as the MacCrimmons who held their land by virtue of their office in the same way as the Beatons, who were the descendants of the hereditary physicians to the Lord of the Isles. There was also a family of Farquarsons, a clan that belonged to the confederacy of Clan Chattan and whose chief's lands were in upper Deeside. The relationship between the feudal superior and the clans resident upon his lands naturally varied with the individuals; for instance Mackintosh and Moray were generally on good terms but upon some occasions they quarrelled and upon one of those occasions it was the leading clansmen who, because the chief was a minor, forced Moray to allow them to remain in occupation of Petty.

The Mackintoshes' relations with Huntly, who had acquired the Lordship of Badenoch, were generally bad and, in their most serious dispute, it was the value of the manpower of the clan that obtained for Mackintosh the restitution of his rights. To summarise, Huntly had achieved the legal murder of Mackintosh in 1550 upon a false charge, and had secured the grant of all his lands to his own son. Mackintosh's relations (including Lord Cassillis) and friends in high places failed to obtain redress, but when the Queen Regent tried to reduce Clan Ranald to obedience and Huntly, in accordance with his feudal obligation, was ordered to proceed against the rebellious clan, his Highland vassals refused to support him and his Lowland ones would not enter such territory. Huntly therefore fell into disgrace. The friends of Mackintosh's heir resumed their efforts and he was re-instated. The story gives a good idea of the impotence of the government and the importance of a numerous and well-armed following. This need continued with little diminution until the legislation after the '45 that abolished rights of heritable jurisdiction and military service.

Of course, many other chiefs of clans (often the founder of the family) held their land directly from the king. MacLeod of MacLeod, for instance, had Royal charters for his lands in Skye and Harris, MacDonald of Sleat, a cadet of the family of the great Lord of the Isles, received a Crown charter for his lands in that vanished Lordship, and, above all, there were the two colossi who swelled into their preponderance during the sixteenth and seventeenth centuries, the Campbells earlier, and later the Mackenzies.

In all those clans, provision was made for younger sons by leases of pieces of land and occasionally, in the case of newly acquired land, by feus. An extremely complex social pattern evolved as families prospered, or increased, or died out. There were good and poor marriages with members of other clans for, within certain territorial limits, the Highlanders were mobile and there was no in-breeding. There are histories with genealogical data for most clans, and Register House is the citadel from which most of the maze of information is derived. To try to trace the collaterals of one's own family as well as one's direct ancestors is a good illustration of the complexity. I am infinitely grateful to Mr George Dixon, an expert in the art, for doing this for me. It was, of course, widely carried on by Highland people who in the past, in this society of infinite variation and close connection, could spot an individual's position to the ninth degree of accuracy. In Strathspey and Badenoch, old maps show a string of the names of farms and one could trace the name of the family that occupied each of them and its relationship to some of the others. This is equally true both in Strathspey below Craigellachie, on the land held by the Laird of Grant, and in Badenoch above it, where the tenure was quite different. So far as I know, it is equally true of almost any other Highland district.

The reason why these cadets and their families remained upon the land and were encouraged to do so is the fact, fundamental to Highland history, that from about the twelfth century onwards, the differences between the Highlands and Lowlands had steadily become accentuated. It is general knowledge that the old language and culture persisted and the distinctive Highland dress was evolved. But such characteristics were but the indications of a fundamentally different way of life. In the Lowlands the feudal obligation to render military service gradually fell into disuse. In the Highlands it remained most actively in force and it was supplemented by the spirit of clannishness, a new development that was possibly the revival of a remote but innate tribal instinct. For survival in a perpetual state of raids and warfare, every clan depended upon its manpower. There was no encouragement to go out into an alien world where being a Highlander would be a heavy handicap and every inducement to stay at home and defend the family home and livestock or raid those of the enemies of the clan. The situation was completely to change during the first half of the eighteenth century and the abolition of 'ward-holding' – the feudal due of armed service – after 1746 was the dramatic climax. It must, however, be emphasised that the value of clan's fighting force did not depend merely upon numbers – it was not a rabble of peasantry – but upon the quality of the armaments and weapons. The absence of mounted forces and the difficulty of obtaining the most effective contemporary weapons (armour in the old days, firearms in the new) had told against the Highlanders ever since medieval times, as the old accounts of actual engagements make plain. Only the relatively better-off could afford the body armour of earlier times or the firearms of later ones. Sir Walter Scott in his account of the Jacobite army in *Waverley* gives a graphic and well-informed account of the varying equipment of the clansmen according to what they could afford. The downhill charge, so skilfully used by Montrose and Dundee, helped for a time to palliate the limited number of clansmen who could afford the accoutrements required for the current battle tactics, but with improved firepower and the development of battle tactics designed to counter such a charge it became a costly failure, as was dismally demonstrated at Culloden. That battle came at the closing of the epoch in which the gentry of the clan were an important asset. But it came at a time when they themselves were finding new outlets and when of their own accord they were abandoning their divided and sub-divided holdings.

As well as abolishing ward-holding in the wake of the '45, Parliament also proscribed the carrying of arms and even the wearing of Highland dress. The latter two were not lasting prohibitions. The abolition of ward-holding was. The military structure of Highland society collapsed and the relationship between the chief and his clansmen was radically changed. To this end 'The Clearances' and the elimination of the tacksman can largely be attributed.

The position of the chiefs was diminished and the bonds of clanship relaxed. Brought into closer contact with the higher standards of the south, most of the chiefs were in some financial difficulty and many of them sold their estates and emigrated. Nevertheless they were important as still forming the focus of local society. Some of them, like Grant of Grant and Mac-Dougall of MacDougall, were leading agricultural reformers. They could give valuable aid by using their influence to obtain commissions and nominations for young clansmen to enable them to start their careers. They still exercised a wide hospitality. Johnson and Boswell have left us some wonderful word pictures of the easy, affectionate respect with which the country people treated them. Johnson was moved by the fervour with which a Maclean living upon Iona exclaimed that 'he would cut his bone for his Chief', although Iona had been lost by the Macleans to the Campbells. As I have shown the influence of this period in the late eighteenth and early nineteenth century playing a strong role in the evolution of the arrangement and plenishings of the typical old-fashioned Highland cottages. Perhaps one illustration of the survival of the old clan spirit under more modern conditions may be quoted – the Grant raid on Elgin in 1820, of which an account by one of its leaders, my grandfather, Sir Patrick Grant, is printed in the first volume of Fraser's *Chiefs of Grant*.

As the years passed after the collapse of the '45, the lesser gentry became redundant not only as followers of the chiefs but in helping to administer a land where, for so long before it, the King's Writ had not run and local administration had been dependent upon the ability of the chiefs to carry it out. Economically also, their usefulness was largely phased out as economic changes spread over the Highlands. The great cattle-droving trade, in which they were an important link, gradually died out and in the demand for grain during the Napoleonic Wars many of them converted the shielings that they had rented into small arable farms. As the new methods of agriculture spread, the tacksman farming a large farm with the help of joint sub-tenants became an anachronism. Forbes of Culloden, acting as factor to the Duke of Argyll, was especially and early opposed to the system and among the tacksmen generally incurred a very bad name. Fortunately for themselves, at the same time a large number of the lesser gentry were becoming dissatisfied with their low standard of living, which became increasingly apparent to them as they made closer contact with the outside world and were taking advantage of the wide range of opportunities that became available during the course of the eighteenth century. There was a gradual increase in contact with the south, not only with the Lowlands of Scotland but with England. Seeing how much higher the standard of living was there encouraged a number of them to live beyond their means in an attempt to adopt a similar life-style. The urgent need for more money was a radical factor in Highland history of the times. It was responsible for the disappearance of a high proportion of the families of the Highland gentry of all degrees. Fortunately for them, many ways of escape from the narrow resources of their native land were open to them. The Union of the Parliaments in 1707 gave them access to more rewarding openings overseas. They, and many ordinary clansmen, sought their fortune in the East, in the service of the East India Company, and in the British colonies in America, including the West Indies, where I happen to know a number of young men from the eastern Highlands did remarkably well for themselves, among them a distant relative of my own. The number of adventurous souls who made careers in the Lowland towns and even in London was greatly increased. Finally, in the second half of the eighteenth century, service in the British Army gave the greatest opening of all for Highlanders of all ranks. The family pedigree and traditions and a few old letters from my own forebears have their counterparts in those of other families in the same position, with numbers of sons sent overseas, many of whom died young in the extremely unhealthy conditions of life in the tropics.

Strathdearn gives a very interesting illustration of the sort of holding some members of the lesser Highland gentry used to have because, unlike those on many estates who held their land only by wadset or lease, they had been able to get feus from the superior, the Earl of Moray, and so had permanent tenure (which they certainly would not have been able to enjoy had they not all been members of Clan Mackintosh or of clans closely allied to it). Until about 25 years ago, the marches of most of them had not much changed. The rough hillsides (now, as grouse moors, the most valuable parts of the properties) were then of little use but we know that several of them contained two and a half ploughgates of arable land, so one assumes that this was regarded as an average portion for a comfortably-off gentleman of the period. A M Mackintosh, in his painstaking history of Clan Chattan, gives the bare facts of the disappearance of the families. Many left because they got into financial difficulties at home, took up other professions, mainly the army and law, and eventually sold their land.

We are very fortunate in having three first-class contemporary accounts of Highland society in the late eighteenth and early nineteenth centuries, written during the period of change, while many of the lesser country gentlemen still remained in the Highlands – those of Doctor Johnson and of Boswell about life in the west, and *Memoirs of a Highland Lady* by Elizabeth Grant for the east. They make delightful reading about a set of interesting people but I do not think that we generally realise how deeply we are indebted to this particular group of Highlanders or how regrettable it is that no special collection of memorabilia specifically connected with them has been formed. Bilingual, they kept alive songs, traditions, standards of conduct. My own old forebear's farming account book is a record of a most primitive system of agriculture systematically recorded in a careful eighteenth-century handwriting. Many of them were truly men of the world who had gone forth to make their way under all sorts and kinds of conditions and yet had kept their love of and pride in the old ways of their people as a living force to be preserved and yet adapted to their new way of life. And they did not act merely as individuals. The habit of these exiled Highlanders of getting together and forming a society was proverbial. The main object of such societies was of course social, though they also did valuable work in helping less fortunate members. But we, as the descendants of their members, are specially indebted to them for preserving and adapting Highland dress and music for use in present-day society of all grades as an aristocratic inheritance and not as an 'Oldie-Worldie' peasant survival. Of all these societies, the Highland Society of London, founded in 1778, is specially well known for the part it played in the Ossianic controversy and for thus preserving for us a precious heritage of ancient Gaelic manuscripts. With other societies, it also did valuable work in preserving Highland piping and (less generally recognised) also in the standardising of the best forms of Highland dancing and dress. In this the Highland regiments also did invaluable service. Of course in valour, endurance, and high standards of conduct, all ranks in the regiment contributed equally, but to the officers, mainly drawn from the lesser gentry, special credit is due for keeping up the standard of piping. For a long time it was they who defrayed the expenses of the pipe-band and in the officers' mess piobaireachd is always played. There has been not only preservation and standardisation but also adaptation to modern ways of life. To go on living, our great languages have been altered and adapted and surely it must be so with social settings and customs. To me, one of the most thrilling sounds that I can hear is a regimental march played on the pipes and drums. It stirs one to the ancestral roots of one's being, yet, remembering what one has read and learnt, one knows that the pipes only succeeded the clarsach as the most esteemed instrument in the sixteenth century, that regimental marches only came into use with the formation of the Highland regiments in the second half of the eighteenth century and that the happy combination of pipes and drums in a band came even later.

It is rather noteworthy that, with a few exceptions, the Highland gentry both resident and overseas did very little to try to conserve the Gaelic. Of course, the earlier generations of them spoke it themselves – both my grandfathers did (and both of them sometimes wore the kilt) but, although I know that my father's father regretted that his children could not speak it, he had realised the fact that their learning time must be fully taken up in studying more necessary and useful subjects.

The aristocratic tradition about the wearing of the kilt, that it was worn by all and not a peasant dress, has been well upheld by the dwindling race of Highland gentry. It developed a very high standard of craftsmanship. When I was young there was in Inverness a well-known tailor, MacDougall, who finally had a branch shop in London, but kept his Inverness address at the top of his headed note-paper. Mackenzie was well known as a brogue-maker, and there was more than one well-known kilt-maker, while it was claimed for Forbes, the wool-shop, that a letter from Canada addressed, 'Forbes Wool-shop, Scotland', was duly delivered. There were highly skilled craftsmen in other Highland towns and their work was increasingly in demand for the 'country gentleman' type of clothing. These included knickerbockers, hand-knit hose and brogues that the rich men in the late Victorian period donned when they came to enjoy the costly deer forests and grouse moors, to the great financial benefit of the Highland proprietors and the many local folk who got from them some well-paid temporary work.

The sense of style that the Highland gentry had maintained contributed materially to the fashion element that brought a most valuable source of wealth to the Highlands at the very time of the great agricultural depression. Nowadays all has changed. Mass-produced goods have replaced the products of these skilled craftsmen, the rich men no longer can bring a domestic staff to enjoy temporary residence in the Highlands, and moors and forests are no longer let in the same way. Country sporting wear consists of jeans and 'wellies' and the kilt is little seen except as a ceremonial dress at weddings (often hired for the occasion), for wear by all and sundry with little real Highland connection. I never thought of the matter when I was making my museum but as the period recedes I feel more and more strongly that a great deal more should be done to record the part that the Highland gentry played from the aftermath of the '45 down to the fundamental break with the impact of the twentieth century World Wars. We have passed the phase when Victoriana was only looked upon as old-fashioned, cluttered up rubbish. Examples of typical ornaments in the fine craftsmanship of the period could be shown, but they would have to be exhibited with some sense of history. In the old days, one belonged to a clan, and one did not collect associations, but a particularly skinny little woman, examining rather a large kilt brooch with the chief's crest surrounded by a strap and buckle to signify that the wearer was his retainer (as is duly laid down by the Lyon Court) remarked, 'I have the right to wear the badge of nine clans'. One could exhibit maps showing the names of the old farms and get some devoted enthusiast (it would never have been me) to search out the pedigrees of their former owners. But the cost of further development would be prohibitive, for the ideal start for such an exhibition would be a room furnished with what a bygone Mrs MacLeod of MacLeod called her 'paraphernalia', the furniture and fittings which came into use as the Highland gentry began to mingle with the rest of the world and which were adapted and copied by the country people. One could display contemporary pictures showing the adaptation of the kilt and the changes in its accessories, for instance, the appearance and disappearance of the Glengarry, and the beauty and the distinction of Highland dress. Of course, it is fairly widely known that the old typical Highland dress was the belted plaid, formed of a double width of material. It is a matter of debate when the kilt was introduced. One can only be thankful that it did take the place of the belted plaid for, although this was a splendid garb for the hard, wild life of the old days, it could not have survived as a convenient dress in more sophisticated times. I saw an amusing example of this fact. I went to a function in Edinburgh and saw one or two men wearing the kilt and looking very odd. It seemed all the more deplorable to me because the Grant tartan with its light blue over-checks is easy to pick out and I recognised it. I also recognised its wearer and he said to me with a pleasant smile, 'You'll be specially interested to see me wearing the old feileadh mór put on in the traditional way' (that is, he had laid a belt on the ground, arranged the double width of plaiding in pleats above it, lain down on top and fastened the belt round his waist. He had then pinned the edges of the width of stuff above the belt together at his shoulders). He added that as he was very fond of walking in the Cairngorms, he had chosen Grant tartan. I could only murmur that he really ought to be exhibited in a museum and I thought to myself that I would gladly immure him in the remotest gallery of the Antiquarian Museum.

One wonders how much does clan spirit still survive today. That, of course, depends upon circumstances. The chiefs of many of the clans are now landless and live outwith the Highlands. In some cases the family ties with the line of descent have been much broken. In the old days, the chief of one's clan was usually associated with the holder of one's land. Nowadays the majority of clansmen live outside the old lands of their clan – very often even outside their native country – and, at the same time, the local people's real love of and pride in their own strath or island survives and not infrequently includes no great opinion of the closest to it, an antagonism that is also a survival. If one has written the history of a clan, one has a certain amount of the documentary evidence, so dear to the academic mind; of the existence of clan feeling in the form of letters inviting one, upon very sparse information, to trace the correspondent's pedigree. Common sense and not bookish learning enabled one to attach very different values to the motives of the writers. Those vary from a very genuine and touching wish to make good old ties, to a simple desire to be one up upon the neighbouring farm. I blessed the Scots Ancestry Research Society as I acknowledged such letters. One piece of evidence of the survival of clan feeling that completely took me by surprise was the importance that so many people attach to tartans. I was, of course, well aware of the important pioneer research of Mr Telfer Dunbar and I did not attach great importance to the exact setts of tartan until I moved the museum to Kingussie and then I only stuck a few pieces of tartan stuff upon a wall. One of them was a well-woven fabric and the colours were mellow and blended well together, and other was of cheap-looking materials and the colours were strident. I only meant to show the good and bad qualities that can go to the making of tartan fabrics. These samples, however, aroused great interest. People eagerly identified their tartan if it was there and asked the reason if it was not. People showed genuine interest and pleasure in it. A charming couple from Australia with a Scots but not Highland name told me that they had been to many shops and had failed to find a tartan of their own but they added, 'We've so much enjoyed seeing the Museum with you that we'll buy some of your tartan and wear it'. It was a pretty compliment, but not to the didactic value of the disquisition that I had just given. I am delighted to think that in the Macdonald Museum at Armadale Castle in Skye, clan associations and examples of the people's bygone material settings are both shown. I was forced to try to make and show a collection of tartans but as clothes rationing was in force it was not at all easy to get hold of bits of fabric. It was a very poor collection but it showed the glimmerings of a theory that James Scarlett, himself a superb weaver of tartan, has worked out which demonstrated the idea that there were basic district types of setts.

This bald narrative can only give an indication of how totally different was the historical background of the Highlanders from that of any peasant society. Its effect on the character and manners of the people has persisted and can be traced down to the present day. It was because of it, and that it is mine, that I ever thought of making *Am Fasgadh*.

19

Laggan

I LOOK back upon my first summer at Laggan as the happiest one that I spent looking after the museum. It was pleasant to live in a house of my own after several years mainly spent in hotels. I much preferred being in the country to life in a tourist centre or in a village. My ménage ran very smoothly and I had congenial friends to stay. Blissfully unaware of the catastrophe that was soon to threaten the museum, I spent happy hours setting out my collection in its new more spacious quarters. The local people were friendly and welcoming and they were to show themselves most sympathetic in the time of anxiety that was to follow. I think that we were consciously savouring the delights of peace because of the brief respite from anxiety that had followed Munich had worn off and a show-down of some kind seemed to become more and more inevitable.

This pleasant time came to an end and arrangements were being made for the evacuation of children from the larger towns and to my horror I was given to understand that the church building that I had just acquired would be requisitioned for storing some of their belongings. I wrote in protest to the officials of the local authority. I sent urgent letters to everyone who I thought had any influence, appealing for their help, but I was again given to understand that a collection such as mine had little hope of consideration in this crisis in the affairs of the nation. I wrote another batch of letters and weary and depressed went outside for a breath of fresh air. It was a clear, still, moonlight night. I went into the church. Shafts of moonlight slanted through the big windows. The pale, selective light gave an austere dignity to the simple shapes of the homely implements and utensils. It surrounded them with an aura of the mystery of time and timelessness. Quite suddenly I felt that the collection had an entity of its own and was not merely an assemblage of my possessions and that it had the will to survive. Ever since then I have been aware of this separate entity. I have watched how other people have reacted to it. Some who were very sympathetic to me have been antipathetic to it. With many more it was the reverse. That night it was a liberating thought. Feeling free of any taint of possessiveness I felt that as the servant and the guardian of the collection, I would go to any length in its defence.

Within a few days I heard that the chairman of Inverness County Council, Cameron of Lochiel, was to be in the neighbourhood and that he was coming to see me. I do not know if he realised that he was entering the lair of a tigress at bay, in defence of her cubs. I said all that I could. He said very little. I told him that as a last resort I would make a pyre of the collection and invite the editor of every paper in Scotland to send a representative to see me set it alight. He said virtually nothing. He left without making any commitment but, after his visit, the plan for storing evacuees' belongings at Laggan was dropped and I heard not a word further about it.

I assured myself that all was well and as there seemed to be no local opening for me to do War work, I made the collection as secure as I could, shut up the house and went south to look for a job. My old mentor and employer, now Sir Henry Clay, found me one at the Institute of Economic Research.

Of course, my life in London has nothing to do with the story of *Am Fasgadh* but as this is a very personal narrative and I have been at pains to indicate something of the history that is a background to the things in the collection and as I was in London at a most historic time, perhaps it would not be out of place to mention the three incidents that stay most vividly in my memory of that time. The first was just after I got to London. It was, of course, during the 'Phoney War' period. I happened to be in a bus driving down Piccadilly. I was watching some people strolling in a leisurely fashion in the Green Park when the sirens sounded, I think for almost the first time. The people in Green Park went on strolling. A woman in the bus asked, 'Oughtn't we to do something about it?', and no one bothered to answer her. It was the typical reaction.

At the height of the Battle of Britain, after work I was making for King's Cross Station to go to Cambridge, from which at the time I was commuting. There was a general feeling of excited exultation. The newspaper boys were constantly changing their news-sheets upon which the latest total of enemy aircraft brought down was scrawled, just as the latest total of runs were written up during an important match of cricket. Just as I got to the right platform at the station, a siren went and the passengers were all herded away from the great glass roof of the building. Everyone was good tempered and helpful, luggage and children were carried, a lame man was helped along, the latest editions of the newspapers were passed from hand to hand. We were only allowed back on the platform just as the train was about to start. Everyone was good tempered in scrambling in. Some of us only managed to get into the guard's van. He did the honours. He arranged the luggage as seats for some people. Others he waved towards the rear window, telling us we would get a good view of 'the aerial combat' from it. All day long, the valour and skill of the pilots of the Royal Air Force had smashed attack after attack by the Luftwaffe and it seemed to me that the spontaneous kindliness of all the people round about me had in its small way the same spirit of defiance of Hitler's cruel tyranny.

By great good fortune I had been given a ticket of admission to the Strangers' Gallery in the House of Commons upon a day when Churchill spoke. The Chamber was more than half empty, members lounged in attitudes of unutterable boredom. A backbencher was on his feet droning away. One of the attendants whispered to us in the Gallery that the Prime Minister 'would soon be up'. Our nerves tingled with anticipation. Quite suddenly and silently the Chamber below became filled to overflowing. In the hush of intense expectancy a small, pale man in the Treasury Bench stood up. His hard, resonant voice seemed to sweep across the Chamber like a great wave at flood tide. Doubts, fears, forebodings were submerged by the intensity of his convictions that our cause was worthy of the uttermost human effort and that it would prevail.

Of course, while working in London, I seized every opportunity to pay a flying visit to Laggan to see how the museum was getting on, to go over the wooden things with anti-woodworm stuff and sprinkle the woollens with anti-moth crystals. I was, however, becoming more and more concerned for the safety of the collection because the district was becoming full of strangers. To meet the demand for timber, the great plantings about Loch Laggan were being felled. The bulk of the work was done by Newfoundlanders, locally known as 'Newfies'. They were strangers and one did not know much about them. At the same time, the Hydro-Electric Board was erecting a dam across the head waters of the Spey. The district was full of talk about the goings-on at the workmen's camp. Most of the men were Glasgow-Irish and of course in war-time labour was scarce and mostly not of high quality. I was warned to keep the door locked and the windows snibbed but I had quite a pleasant contact with them. On one of my brief visits to Laggan, I was busy inside the museum when a large party of them appeared. They were evidently having a look round the country and had obviously taken of refreshment. They wanted to know what was inside the church. I treated them with the most formal politeness and invited them to come inside. They were delighted. They recognised some of the farm implements as the very same they'd seen their 'Da's' use. Some were almost moved to tears. They insisted upon having a whip-round for the benefit of the museum. We parted the best of friends. All the same, I was extremely worried.

At this time, my job in London was keeping an indexed summary of entries in the Press upon current economic events for Sir Henry Clay and Mr J Maynard Keynes. Mr Maynard Keynes has played so important a part in politico-economic thinking that although I worked directly under Henry Clay's direction and only made brief contacts with Mr Keynes, it is worthwhile to record the impression that he made upon me. He said very little although he was pleasant and courteous. His face was not at all what one would have expected as that of a great and original thinker and an active patron of the arts. For instance, his eyes, which were dark, looked curiously opaque. They did not light up when he spoke of what was obviously of interest to him. Henry Clay, for whom I had worked and with whom I was upon pleasant master and pupil terms, was interested in hearing about my efforts to form and maintain the museum and was sympathetic over my anxieties for its safety. It was due to his influence that I was allowed to do so much of my work by post and away from London. I am deeply grateful to him, to Mr Keynes and to the authorities of the Institute for Economic Research for this permission. It entailed a good deal of travelling. Otherwise it was ideal for me for it enabled me to keep up an appearance of occupation at Laggan and at the same time do War work that I found very interesting.

As things turned out, all unknowingly, I had moved the museum from Iona at the right time because, during the War, Iona was declared to be a 'prohibited area' and I would have had difficulty in getting to and fro to look after the collection. I had, however, only made the move to Laggan as a temporary expedient and I was still 'keeping an eye out' for something ideal for its permanent quarters. I was particularly glad to have the chance of exploring possibilities in the central Highlands because the traditional social organisation and the distribution of land survives in many districts there and has been lost in the crofting areas. A considerable amount of oral tradition still survives there and there is a greater sense of continuity with the past. I heard of various possibilities including a disused slaughterhouse. I was so much attracted by the account of a disused school near Crieff that I snatched time to go and look at it. It would, however, have been too costly to adapt. I would have loved to have bought a very fine old farmhouse in Badenoch with an eventful past but I found that I should have had to take over a stock of sheep as well. Finally, I was told of a disused woollen mill at Kingussie. I have grown up with a considerable respect for the tantrums of Highland burns and the Gynack is a large and vigorous specimen. I did not fancy it as too near a neighbour and in other respects the place was not suitable, but the agent who was arranging the sale and who turned out to be Mr Petty, the town clerk of Kingussie, and who was to be one of the museum's best and kindest friends, then mentioned that there was another house for sale that might interest me. I went to see it. It was the old shooting lodge and was still called 'The Lodge'. It was accessible and the building was well adapted for my purpose. There was about the right amount of land around it. Kingussie is in the middle of the Highlands, neither east nor west coast, and was a good tourist centre, but at that time, the development at Aviemore as a sports centre was undreamed of and when I decided to buy 'The Lodge' I made a far, far better choice of a site for the museum than I ever dreamed.

20

Kingussie

SINCE I gave it up, the museum has been so much enlarged and changed that it may be of a little interest to describe the early lay-out.

The hall was large and the staircase wide and of easy access so I included it in the area I opened to the public, which also included the whole of the upper floor. The lower floor I used as my residence and for storing things. My housekeeper, also the general factotum to the museum, occupied a separate wing at the end of the house. The heraldic shields, made for the Inverness Exhibition, decorated the hall. I did not display these shields so prominently merely because they were most ornamental, but because they symbolised the devotion to their chief and the pride in their clan that formed so important an element in the lives of the Highlanders in the old days. Along the wall was the one purpose-built showcase I could afford to buy. It contained the ornamental snuff boxes, toddy ladles, pieces of jewellery and other treasures that are such an important element in the relics of the old Highland way of life. And equally precious, a few examples of the fine, beautifully coloured fabrics woven of combed yarn.

Upstairs, a small room on the right held my sporting and fishery exhibits. I am afraid that the sea fishery part was the weakest in the whole museum although it had a very attractive model of a fishing boat. There was, however, one exhibit that gave me a lot of amusement. It was an old poaching device known as an 'otter'. It consisted of a piece of wood with fishing flies or hooks on a cast attached to it. The poacher set it afloat on a piece of water on the side from which the wind was blowing and then went round and collected it when it had been blown across, with such fish as had been foolish enough as to take the flies or baited hooks. Most visitors passed it guilelessly by. A few older ones would give me a very knowing look. They were far too discreet to ask me how I had got it.

The big room to the front had rather a mixture of things. Among examples of crafts and tools was rather a full collection of tinkers' implements, which the tinkers regularly brought their children to see. Though they were friendly they never described how the horn was softened so as to be shaped into a spoon in a mould. Old men have told me that when they were boys they were sometimes told to take a cow's horns to the tinkers to be made into spoons. The tinkers would tell them to go away and come back to collect the spoons. They were never allowed to see the process of manufacture, afraid that the carefully kept secret might have been discovered. But I rather suspect that the art has been lost and that it was due to ignorance that the present-day tinkers would not say. Among other tools that I had was an early set of shoemaker's tools and a thrawcrook, a tool used for twisting straw rope which was easily made but not strong. Heather rope was much stronger. No tools were used to make it and it was twisted by hand. I had one unique example of rope made from tree roots and I had ropes made of horse-hair. This was a scarce commodity. If a pony with a long tail was stabled in an inn it was liable to lose it. I had, also, a horse-hair fowling rope from St Kilda, where no young man was supposed to marry until he had secured one because it was essential for life on the island. I had a horse-hair band for tying a cow's hind legs together if she was being milked in the open. This would be carefully kept because it would enable anyone with evil powers to steal the cow's milk. I was rather proud to be able to show several charm stones with the method of working cures with them. I also kept there my small collection of books. I had an Irish Gaelic translation of the Book of Common Prayer and several Gaelic Bibles.

It is a disgrace to the Church and the authorities that no Gaelic version of the New Testament was published till 1767 and of the Old Testament till 1783-1801, although an Irish version had been available since 1685. I had not a copy of the first edition but it was touching to see how the edges of the pages of later editions of the Bible that I had were worn by so much turning, and the covers carefully replaced by home-made ones.

The walls of all the rooms were more or less covered by notes that I had written up of relevant traditions, proverbs, working songs or other details. People were often much interested in old inventories, or notes of the prices of things, or in reproductions of old prints or pictures. I feel that this was very important, especially in a collection of things interesting and important not for their outward beauty but because of their association with a way of life in the past. In this particular room I had written up a list of the things that it was lucky or unlucky to do on each day of the week and during certain quarters of the moon. It only too often gave one a splendid reason for not doing some tiresome job that was nagging at one's conscience.

Two rooms down the corridor were devoted to textiles. Marjory Kendon set up a loom. There were various utensils for the preparation of the yarn and there were the examples of the dyes that had been made for the Inverness Exhibition. There was also a large iron pot about two feet high, which was used for dyeing. I did, however, keep one spinning wheel in the hall where there was more room so that I could demonstrate how it worked and I generally spun with a spindle as I was showing people round the museum. That end of the museum reeked of various preparations guaranteed to discourage moths because I also had on display some of my home-made blankets. I learnt to my cost that moths much prefer home-spun woollens to the woollens processed in a factory. Along that corridor I also had a collection of photographs of the local types of Highland cottages.

The other front room and another beyond it contained furniture and household plenishings. I had several babies' cradles. The hoods were of two distinct types. One of them was more elaborate than the other. This was not a district variation but I think that it showed how the styles that the gentry copied from the south became adapted by the homelier people. When showing these cradles, I had an illustration of how quickly old ways are dying out in the Highlands. A party of schoolchildren from Laggan came to see the museum and asked me what the cradles were used for. In some surprise I replied, 'for holding babies'. The children were puzzled and said that surely the babies would drown. It turned out they thought the cradles were tanks. Rather a bossy lady (I happened to know she was the wife of a professor) once gave me a grand opening for expounding my pet theories about Highland furniture. She was personally conducting a group of subservient friends round the museum and when they got to these rooms she exclaimed that the furniture was not at all Highland; one chair was Chippendale, another Hepplewhite and the table was Empire. Needless to say I gave them chapter and verse of my own views. Most of the furniture had reached the museum as the result of changing fashions in the furnishings of the 'front parlour' and I hope that the museum did not represent the frigid formality of many of those apartments.

A room off the left-hand corridor I devoted to musical instruments. Heloise Russell Fergusson, the harpist, most generously gave me a fine clarsach. It was made of several different woods and if it was not very old it was a most excellent copy. She said she did not wish it to be played on, but before I consigned it to silence in a glass case I could not resist sweeping my fingers across the strings. It had a most beautiful mellow tone. The modern clarsachs are copies of very ancient instruments. They are similar to one carved upon a mediaeval grave-slab in Kintyre. But I wonder if the wandering poets and minstrels who were such a feature of Highland life in the fifteenth century carried instruments that were as heavy and had as many angles wherewith to bump one. A friend of mine, Eleanora Cameron, used to sing and play the clarsach at the meetings of various Highland Gatherings in London and I sometimes acted as her minstrel boy. I used to pity Scott's orphan boy who, in the Lay of the Last Minstrel, carried the harp of the minstrel 'infirm and old' as I lugged that clarsach down the stairways of the underground and onto buses. The glass case into which I put the clarsach had once contained a stuffed bird. Very fortunately for me the fashion for having such things was going out and I was able to buy two or three at local roups. Specially made show-cases are very expensive and although I did not like incarcerating my exhibits, one had to take this precaution for a few things. I had a set of bagpipes, a 'trump' (jew's harp) which was used for playing dance music and a precentor's tuning fork, and of course there was scope for a great deal of written material, from the notation of pipe music to the 'repeating' method, a special way of singing the psalms, etc.

The large room at the end of the corridor was devoted to the display of utensils for cooking and lighting. Simple as they were and mainly made from whittled wood, not one of the utensils, ladles or bowls was exactly like another. One liked to think of the pride and ingenuity of the makers and I arranged several specimens of each group not only to demonstrate this but because I think that a crowded setting, like that which had been their home, was more suitable for them.

I was able to buy a large wooden hut for the agricultural implements, which made a suitable setting for them. A good many of these obviously went back to the period before steel was made and cast-iron became easily available and the prime exhibit was a wooden plough, small and suitable to the Highland four-horse plough team. It came from Abriachan, high above Loch Ness.

Things look so much more at home if not imprisoned in glass cases but, as I had discovered in Iona days, visitors, if they are really interested, have a maddening habit of picking things up and putting them down in another place. 'DO NOT TOUCH' notices, however large they are, are quite ineffectual. Besides the risk of damage, the poor curator goes through agonies of anxiety when she misses the thing in its accustomed place and before she discovers it somewhere else. I was rather proud of my plan to discourage the moving of exhibits. I got some fine wire and looped it round each exhibit as it stood on display, so that if one were moved the next ones would be disturbed. Anyone who touched the things got a fright and any attempt at stealing would be prevented. It is a credit to our visitors and also to us as custodians that we did not lose a single thing by theft.

I kept everything very simple for reasons of economy, but in any case, such a background suited the homely things and I hope that it encouraged the visitors who to me were more welcome than any others, the country people. Once when I was showing a couple round, the woman was not paying much attention – 'Janet', said the man, 'Why will you not stop looking out of the window and look at what the lady is showing you?' 'It's the ducks', she replied. We had a chat about my runner ducks, a breed she had not seen. Then we passed on to other things and I learnt more from them than they did from me. I think that the very small-scale farming that I did in order to feed my livestock and to use the fields that went with the house, was of real value in giving a country feel to the museum.

I am now so crippled that I have not been able to see all the ingenious audio-visual devices that are now used and so I cannot know how I should react to them. Personally, I feel a strong distaste to the use of artificial figures as they always seem to me to be like stuffed human beings. And I also feel that to exhibit anything in lighting which is quite different in intensity from that in which it was made and was used and to isolate it from its accustomed setting is rather like putting a criminal in the pillory. On the other hand I feel that it is of the greatest help to the appreciation of the exhibits to provide as much background information as one possibly can by pictures, maps and written matter of anecdotes, bills of sales, descriptions of the methods of use and anything else that one can think of. I found that such information was much appreciated, often quite unexpectedly.

One day, which happened to be a holiday in Dundee, a rather rough-looking trio from there – a woman and two men – came to Kingussie and visited the museum. Two of them were bored and left almost at once, calling to the third to come with them. He was avidly reading some of the notices on the walls and replied, 'Oh! Get to Hell out of this. Can't you see that I am enjoying myself?' I found that he was reading some translations of Gaelic verse in the classic metres.

To create a masterpiece that is a delight to men and women of all sorts is an achievement rarely attained in any of the arts. In making a museum, as in the very pedestrian branch of literature, writing books of instruction, it is essential to bear in mind the sort of people one is trying to cater for. Although a good museum should try to be all things to all men, nevertheless I think one should have one's priorities in the kind of public one is seeking to serve. Mine, of course, were my own Highland people. As an assistant (who often played a leading role) in looking after the Folk Museum, the grounds, the livestock and also the house itself, I had a housekeeper, Mrs Myra Grant. She had very good taste with a background knowledge of Highland country ways acquired as the daughter of a Skye crofter and wife of a shepherd. She had the old Highland charm and shrewdness. She lived with her family in the wing at the end of the house. For extra work, such as showing people round the museum and heavier work outside, I was able to get part-time helpers from the village. One of the best was a schoolboy called Puck Ross. He seemed to me the embodiment of the real country-man with all his innate skills and instincts. With great tact and efficiency he initiated me into such tasks as binding sheaves and making hay coils. The museum received very willing service from these helpers although, in the time of pressure after the War, it was not always easy to get men for some of the manual tasks. Just one, not a permanent resident in Kingussie, was most irritatingly dilatory in building a haystack. I said to Mrs Grant that I did not know how to get him to get a move on. She said might she, as a married woman, give me a piece of advice. I begged her to do so. She said the way to get a man to work was to admire him. I begged her to go and admire the man. Presently I went to see how the stack was getting on. The hay was piled high and sweat was pouring down the man's face and arms as he tossed up great pitchfork-fuls of it. Mrs Grant was standing with her hands clasped gazing up at him. As I came up to her she turned her head, gave me a wink, and then resumed her pose of admiration. I left them to it.

The work of hay-making and presence of livestock played an important part in giving a homely feel to the museum and a lived-in feeling to the cottages I was to build. I started off with sheep. I was very anxious to get some of the old Highland breed of sheep which had survived upon St Kilda but I did not succeed in obtaining any. Instead, I had some of the wild sheep from the island of Soay. These lovely little beasts with the finest of wool could outrun any collie and jump most fences. The man from whom I bought my first ewes had said 'Food is best fence', and they soon became delightfully tame. To mate with them, the directors of Edinburgh Zoo presented me with a Soay tup. For months he would not move beyond a space about a dozen yards square. I suppose that was the size of his old enclosure. Later on, to prevent inbreeding, I exchanged young stock with a Mr Storey who kept a flock of Soay sheep in Norfolk.

From the moment I had a place to build cottages in the tradi-tional styles, I longed to be able to pasture Highland cattle around them. Just after the War there was rather a fashion for raising Highland cattle on hilly pastures and for crossing them with other breeds. I despaired of getting any. Sheriff Grant of Rothiemurchus, whose whole family was immeasurably helpful to me, heard of my wish. He had a fine herd of Highlanders and he said that he would let me have two stirks very cheaply but that I must choose them myself. I hurried off to Rothiemurchus but my enthusiasm had been much tempered by gloomy warnings by neighbours of the restlessness of Highland cattle and their proclivity for jumping fences or scrambling through them and I was painfully aware that my fencing was old and rather decrepit. The grieve took me to see a herd of about two dozen stirks. He was evidently prepared for a long technical discussion about the points of the various animals and when I, still concerned over my fences, blurted out the question, which ones were the peaceable and the least likely to jump, his face was a study. As a matter of fact he sold me two little shaggy golden brown beauties that the experts afterwards pronounced to be very good indeed. I cannot resist adding to this another story.

When Edinburgh University bestowed upon me an LLD, the *Scotsman* published a picture of a group of the recipients, Neil Gunn, the well-known author, being one of them. It happened that Mickey, an Irishman who sometimes did odd jobs for me, was doing roadwork near the home of Neil Gunn. As he afterwards told me, he and a local man, a workmate, saw this photograph. They opined there was a lot of grey matter in the heads of the people in it and the local man said that he knew Neil Gunn who had written a power of books. Mickey claimed acquaintanceship with me and not to be outdone said that although he did not rightly know if I had written any books, he could fairly claim that I was born with a grand eye for the points of a cow.

The little Highlanders terrified some of the visitors, especially after they took to making friendly advances in the hope of a tit-bit, and although they never jumped my fences they would poke their heads through to eat the grass on the other side and their horns got entangled in the wires. So eventually I had to part with them and made a good profit. Instead I bought a cow.

In most parts of the Highlands, milk in glass bottles or other containers from large dairies is almost exclusively used. Very few individuals keep milch cows for their own use. Kirstie herself, with the milking stool and pail, was really an exhibit. We kept her in the Lewis cottage byre which gave it a feeling of authenticity. It is amusing to notice how definitely most country people prefer either sheep or cattle. Fortunately Mrs Grant, like me, preferred cattle. If she had not taken charge of Kirstie I would not have adventured upon keeping a cow; and I would have missed a lot, for cows are interesting animals with lots of character. They smell nice and are nice to touch and handle. Even if one keeps the calves, one has a supply of milk for most of the year and the arrival of a calf is a moment of high drama. And one's garden is rich in muck beyond the wildest dreams of most gardeners.

Another of my animals also ranked as an exhibit. The keeping of goats was an important item in old Highland farming and the different groups of present-day Highland wild goats are all descended from domestic goats that escaped to the wild. Griach had been found as a waif and reared by the family of Mr Macdonald, the master-builder of the cottages, and given to me. She was gentle and wily and devastatingly destructive if she got into the garden. Once when two half-breed Dalmation dogs rampaged through my fields and came too near her kid, she tackled first one and then the other and sent them packing with their tales between their legs.

My object in buying some land had been to build some cottages in the traditional local styles. The principle upon which to build them was difficult to decide upon. Scandinavian buildings are largely of wood and brick. The component parts of such buildings can be numbered, taken down and re-assembled and this was the method invariably used in making the folk museums – all the cottages were actually old. It would be difficult to reconstruct old Highland cottages in this way as they were built of dry-stone walling, a minimum of timber and of peat. They were thatched with straw as heather was generally too heavy for the timbers of the roof. None of these materials lent themselves to permanent re-erection. Dry-stone walling depends upon the placing and fitting together of the stones. I only saw one example of a dry-stone building in a folk museum in the Faroe Islands. The building looked a 'rickle' [carelessly piled heaps of stones], so the reconstruction was evidently not very successful. The separate divots of peats which are used as the under layer of the roof or as the upper parts of the walls become solidified into a single mass and the whole roof or top of the wall would have to be removed in one piece or, in the difficult operation of cutting it into sections, it would inevitably crumble. The straw thatch from its very nature would have to be constantly renewed. This was regularly done every year with the thatching of the Long Island. Even in places where, with different methods of thatching, it was more durable, one rarely saw a group of thatched cottages without a man on a ladder putting a patch onto the thatch of one of them.

Of course, even if one used the traditional materials, what was built would be liable to be bogus and theatrical. So I hit upon a third solution to the problem: to find old men who had actually been employed in building cottages of the local traditional style and employ them to build new cottages in the old way. I was delighted with myself for thinking up this plan. I did so because Mr Alexander Macdonald, a man ideal for carrying it out, was my mother's near neighbour and I knew him well. It was only after the work had started that I realised that my solution was not perfect. The use of steel tools, iron nails and sawn timber had come to the Highlands about 150 years earlier. Although they had used traditional ways of building, the materials used in the construction of the houses that they had helped to build were no longer entirely traditional. Nails were used instead of wooden pegs and sawn planks for the woodwork. The building of my cottages was a genuine replica of a period of survival but not of more primitive earlier times. And it is, of course, to this transitional period that the main part of the plenishings of all the more old-fashioned cottages that I visited belonged. Of course, in any case, I would have wanted my first cottage to be built in the local style, that of the Strathdearn and of all the central Highlands, a style in which the main feature was the couples that supported the roof, and I was extremely fortunate that I knew Mr Macdonald and his family well, as he was the very man to build one. He farmed at Balvraid but he was also a dry-stone dyker and he loved that beautiful craft. He warmed to the idea of building a cottage that would be 'the very spit' of the one in which he had been brought up in Glen Urquhart. Mr Petty helped to acquire the ruins of a dyke close by and it was a great joy to watch how skilfully Mr Macdonald selected each stone from a pile and eased it into place as he laid the foundation into which the couples would be planted and the walls built around them. I had hoped to get small trees such as would have been used in the traditional way but the owner of a birchwood from whom I hoped to get them would not let me have them. All the same it was a great thrill to see the sawn timber baulks that I had to get being raised and fastened together and the framework of lighter timber being erected to support the heavy peat roof. The cottage had a 'hanging chimney' and old-fashioned grate and hobs. Mrs Grant chose and arranged the inside furnishings, the sort of things one would expect to find in an old-fashioned little cottage in my very young days. She made a special point of making two arrangements that I had also often noticed in the older houses I had visited when I was collecting. First, if there were children, home-made chairs specially made for them were always there. Second, in a corner a cloth was spread on a little table or kist and on it arranged any little treasures, such as toddy ladles, snuff mulls or something exotic brought back from travels abroad. Mrs Grant afterwards used this room for some tableaux of life in the Highlands which made charming photographs.

The cottage was Mr Macdonald's pride and joy. He sent all of his relatives over to see it and personally cared for its upkeep. He also helped very much in other ways. He found an oldish man from Back in Lewis, who supervised the building of a cottage in the style of the Long Island. I have described how, in a gale of wind, I was able to appreciate how admirably these buildings with their low roofs and double walls were adapted to the climate. This cottage had a hearth in the middle of the floor and we furnished it so far as we could with things that would have belonged to an earlier period.

By the great kindness of a benefactor in Harris, who took infinite trouble in going through the complicated procedure necessary in a crofter township, I was given the grindstone and wooden working parts of a 'clackmill'. This is a very old form of grain mill. The grindstones are not turned by an overshot water-wheel but by a shaft with blades turned directly by a mill stream running below the mill. I put it up close to the Lewis house where there was a slight slope and I hoped that one day I would be able to make a reservoir and on special occasions allow a rivulet to run under the mill but I never got round to this.

After this success I was increasingly unlucky in my building operations. My third cottage was planned to be one of the south-western Highland type and I planned it to be built on a rather more spacious scale so that I could furnish it rather differently. My friends from Iona, Mr and Mrs J MacCormick, came to stay and he made a plan with careful measurements for a cottage of the kind familiar to him. Unfortunately he had calculated for better and more seasoned timber than I was able to get (all this during post-War scarcities). Although Mr Macdonald made a good job of the mason-work, the roof always gave me trouble.

As I had furnished my cottages I could not let people into their rooms. I had, therefore, barriers fixed across the doors over which people could look into the rooms. In the folk museums I had visited, visitors had been able to go inside the cottages, empty except for a few very large articles. This, of course, enabled one to examine the structural details of the buildings, but it gave no idea of what they looked like when people lived in them. There was no evidence of the full life that country people lived in the old days such as one used to see when one actually visited old-fashioned country cottages. I feel this very strongly because it was the visit to the Musée Plantin with its printing presses set ready for work that affected the whole course of my life and led to the building of my cottages about half a century later. I am afraid that very irreverently the sight of the empty cottages in a folk museum made me think of the Parable that likened a man, out of whom a devil had been driven, to a house empty, swept and garnished, which was entered by a band of devils worse than the first. This was rather rude to the next party of tourists whom I watched guilelessly entering the cottage. There is something desolate about an empty, unfurnished room: it is the sight of familiar things within the room of a friend that makes it so welcoming even if he or she is absent. If one finds a stranger there, one resents it. I feel that the presence of 'stuffed human beings' in a reconstructed room is an intrusion distracting from one's sense of the continuity of time and the reality of the people who long ago actually lived and worked there.

A piece of bad luck in my cottage-building efforts occurred soon afterwards. I had had great hopes of securing the couples and other woodwork of a cottage at the Streens in Strathdearn that had fallen vacant. The Rev. Mr MacCuish, by then translated from Iona to Moy, had offered to number the various timbers. A lorry driver was willing to fetch them. Mickey, who had acted as Mr Macdonald's labourer, would have built the dry-stone foundations. Unfortunately, there was a little delay in completing the arrangements. A tramp, spending the night in the cottage, was careless with the dottle of his pipe and set the place alight. A worse disaster followed. During the summer that I was to spend at Kingussie, in a spell of very dry weather, an engine on the railway line was using unusually sparky coal and set the grass alight at several places along the line. One of the sparks landed upon the roof of my beautiful Inverness-shire cottage and even before we could reach it, the roof went up in flames and we could do nothing to save it. I had to break the news to Mr Macdonald. He had aged greatly. He would never be able to build a dry-stane dyke again. We both nearly broke down.

Am Fasgadh, the shelter, was able to save five collections of old Highland things that otherwise would have been dispersed. In describing the scarcity of tools in the past I have already told of the generosity of one friend of the museum in allowing me to take the pick of his collection of country implements. Another collection of a very different kind came to the museum in quite a different way and helped to illustrate the continuance of the fact that life in the Highlands was not a peasant culture. It came from Mrs Lang Rose, due to a family friendship that went back for generations between my mother's people and the Mackintoshes of Farr. One of the last survivors of that family had married a Congreve: her daughter, Dora, although much older, had been a friend of mine. Mrs Lang Rose was her cousin and heiress. It was a family trait not to throw things away and when, by Dora's last wish, I went through her things, I found not only best dresses that went back to the days of bustles, but charming cotton frocks for morning wear of the same period. Even in my young days, when we changed from informal to formal dress more often than now, to be over-dressed was considered almost as great a social gaffe as to be under-dressed, a point I thought was not taken into account in some television period productions. I purchased and housed this collection in a Nissen hut bought for the purpose. I was also able to show a charmingly demure grey frock that belonged to a minister's wife and one of the dresses heavily trimmed with black crêpe in which Victorian society, including country people, showed the exaggerated respect for the memory of the dead. I also showed one of the drugget skirts and a woman's home-spun plaid of combed yarn.

For some time I had been told that Mr J Macdonald, the blacksmith at Nethy Bridge, who had lately died, had made a wonderful collection of old things. Upon further enquiry I learnt that his widow was carefully preserving them in a shed. In her anxiety to conserve them she would not allow anyone to see them. I made a tentative approach through a friend to see if I might look inside the shed but, of course, while they were being preserved as a memorial to her late husband I could not hope to get any of them. Eventually the house and the shed changed hands. I received word that the new owners wished to replace the shed and would allow the museum to have the contents if I came to remove them. Naturally I hurried to Nethy Bridge by the best means available. I no longer had a car. I was taken to the small wooden shed. It was padlocked, but no key was forthcoming and the padlock had to be forced. I stepped inside and my foot went through the floorboards. Fortunately, the flooring was only just above the ground so that one could move about and examine the contents but as I moved one of the chairs it came to pieces in my hands and I was doubtful of the soundness of the other wooden things. As I floundered about various people looked in and asked if the collection was being dispersed. The owner of the shed had been obliging in getting the promise of a lorry to bring home the things I had selected. I was able to choose a number of things but I had to remain on guard until the lorry came to take me and my cargo back to Kingussie.

The fourth good haul that I made stays in my mind because of the beauty of the drive to it. A constant summer visitor to Nethy Bridge with a sixth sense for spotting antiques told me of a recently deceased farmer on Deeside who had collected things and whose family would allow the museum to have the pick of them. There is always something rather exciting in coming to a watershed. I hired a car and we set out and drove along the beautiful side road that climbed through passes in the Cairngorms from Strathspey with its dark plantings and wild forests to where the land begins to slope down again and the high hills dwindled into the foothills of Deeside. We passed beautiful Loch Kinord with its surrounding woods and on arriving at the farm we not only were able to collect some interesting things but we examined a most unusual Pictish stone in the front garden with the symbol of a goose or duck upon it.

The fifth windfall that befell the museum was the generous gift of a collection of curling stones, varying from crudely shaped stones to examples more and more like the conventional highly polished ones of today. Nowadays the game is largely played upon indoor rinks of artificial ice in an urban setting. As a rural sport it is sadly evident that the playing of 'The Roaring Game' has declined, for in many parts of the country one comes across examples of ponds said to have been used for curling. I displayed these stones in a thatched lean-to built against the museum hut, which held the dresses. We tried to imitate the method of thatching intermediate between the Lewis and central Highlands types. It was cheap and it fulfilled three useful purposes.

I opened the museum to visitors during the summer months. I cannot remember the numbers and I handed over my records of visitors and takings from the collection box, but I most vividly remember we had a great variety. We had parties of various kinds. Bus parties often contained foreigners and it is strange how in this short contact certain nationalities appealed to me more than others. I definitely preferred the Dutch. I will not say which appealed to me least. Although they had a pleasant time, I rather question the educational value of indiscriminately carting round large groups of children. On the other hand, when the ground has been well prepared and the visit suits the children's capacities, they somehow are very receptive and it is amusing and worthwhile to show them round. One got a most stimulating response sometimes from the most unexpected quarters. In general, among the more serious visitors, I was surprised at the intensity of their highly charged emotional obsession with 'The Clearances' and the attitude of the Lowlanders who had much condescending pity for the simplicity of the old ways of Highland life but were not so sympathetic when one stressed the ancient, aristocratic and highly cultured origin of Gaelic civilisation.

I was annoyed and humiliated and also financially penalised by the refusal of the authorities to recognise the museum as educational and exempt it from the payment of Entertainment Tax. We had neither the time nor the people available to sort through all the paraphernalia that the local tax officer required if I had made a charge for admission. So I put a collection box at the door. Most people put something into the box but copper coins predominated and I estimated that the contents of the collection box equalled 3d per head of the visitors. One Sunday, an affluent-looking man in a very grand car called and asked to be shown over the museum. Mrs Grant, thinking that the visit might be profitable, did so. As he left, he hunted through a handful of coins, evidently searching for one of the lowest denomination, and said to her, 'What do people generally put in?' She replied, 'Most people give what they can afford!' His donation was in paper money. I protested to the authorities and one visitor whose name I ungratefully forget, who had arranged for groups of school children to come to see the museum and who was, I think, president of the EIS, wrote to the Revenue Authorities but without result. This shabby treatment rankled especially when students, as they often did, said that their professor had told them to visit the museum and to ask me to show them round or elucidate some special problem, or when I got letters requiring detailed replies upon some subject.

A type of visitor that was annoying was almost always feminine. Without any valid reason for not coming at the proper time they tried by the exercise of self-conscious charm to be specially shown round at times when the museum was closed. When I was pointing out to one of them that all museums were closed at fixed times and that staff had regular hours of work, she replied, 'Oh, but you do it voluntarily'. I felt inclined to reply that fools as volunteers were, they had to eat. On the whole, in looking back, I am glad to think that I bore kindly with enquiring students and visitors who for some good reason called to see the museum. I am indeed thankful that I did so to a very shy school boy from Grantown, for he grew up into George Dixon to whose encouragement, kindness and erudition I am immeasurably indebted.

I suppose that my best-known visitor was Aneurin Bevan, who was at the time Minister of the Crown. He, a Welsh Celt (a Brythonic Celt), had wanted to see something of Highland Celts (Goidelic Celts) and in course of his trip attended the Highland Games at Newtonmore. Politically all Celts are not at one. A true-blue Conservative friend told me that when, as was the custom during the evening after the Games, the pipers went round the various hotels. There they played a sprig on the pipes and drank the health of a generous guest who supplied the liquor. At the hotel where Bevan was staying he, as a generous guest, supplied the drinks; the piper, instead of proposing his name, declared, 'I propose the health of Winston Churchill and may the Lord bless him'. Of course, when Mr Bevan visited the museum I received him with great respect as His Majesty's Minister. He was a delightful person to show round. We discussed things freely and although our views upon most subjects were diametrically opposed, he said nothing to wound or antagonise me. He was, of course, a very, very able politician.

Two pieces of most welcome recognition and encouragement came my way and I give thanks for them to the influence of a very good friend to the museum. In 1948 Edinburgh University, as I have mentioned, bestowed upon me the honorary degree of LLD. They entertained me royally when I went to Edinburgh to receive it. It was not only an enjoyable occasion but the right to stick 'Doctor' in front of my surname gave me a little of the status that as an amateur voluntary worker I very much needed. It was a most generous gesture and I have felt grateful for it ever since.

The second nice thing that happened was that in 1950 I was asked to give the Rhind Lectures by the Society of Antiquaries. This was a compliment and a challenge and I spent many happy hours working on my chosen theme – the different periods in Highland history. I spent most of that time in the Central Public Library in Edinburgh behind mounds of books that Miss Dickson and other kind assistants in that most welcoming of libraries piled upon my desk. 'Though I say it as shouldn't', as the saying goes, the lectures went off very well. I specially noticed, at every lecture, the intense concentration upon the face of one of my listeners. I thought it was a look of disapproval, especially as I had to touch upon contentious themes, religious, political and economic. When, after the final lecture, this man came up to me and said he would 'like a word', I rather nervously wondered what was coming, but all he said was, 'I wanted to give you these, I picked them for you in my garden', and he handed me a bunch of flowers. It was one of the nicest things that has ever happened to me. Another nice thing was the fee I received which helped in the financial stringency of financing the museum. I am ashamed to say that although I recognised the obligation to try to publish the lectures, my periodic attempts to do so have all been thwarted. At long last, in partnership with Hugh Gray Cheape, I hope the book will see the light. I am sure I owe the chance of giving these lectures to Mr R B K Stevenson, keeper of the National Museum of Antiquities of Scotland. He was a kind friend to the museum. It is heart-warming to recall the kindness of many other people and among them I feel that the museum owes a very special debt to Mr Petty, Sheriff Grant, his wife and son, and also to some members of the staff of Kingussie School.

As time went on I became increasingly concerned about the future and the financing of the museum. During the years my hopes for my collection had changed. At the beginning my plans had been to provide a shelter for things in immediate danger of destruction, in the hope that someone, somewhere, would eventually form a permanent museum for their preservation. As the collection developed it had acquired, in my mind, a definite entity which I desired to preserve. When, after a good deal of searching, I finally acquired the house and grounds at Kingussie, I had come to feel that this was the most suitable place for it to remain. The problem of financing it, looking after it and providing continuity of guardianship became more and more acute. Less and less did I wish to continue to spend my life indefinitely living in penury and discomfort in a corner of the museum and in a place where I did not wish to settle permanently. Furthermore, there was an element of urgency on the problem because if my health failed or I died, there was no one to take charge of the museum or make arrangements for the future of the collection and no money to provide for this. I approached and went to see a number of individuals and organisations. It was made clear to me that while I owned the buildings and the collection, I could not be eligible for any form of grant. It became equally clear to me that to hand over the management of the museum to an independent committee while I remained financially responsible for the running of the buildings and the land, which represented a considerable part of my private capital, would have been sheer lunacy. We found a stop-gap solution to the difficulty by forming a group termed 'Friends of *Am Fasgadh*', with a committee that would receive grants for the museum. Under this arrangement, Mr Stevenson, who rightly thought the collection ought to have a catalogue, was the main agent in procuring a grant from the Society of Antiquaries of Scotland for this purpose. The more permanent problem of providing for the future of the museum remained, and I became increasingly anxious for release from the responsibility for it. Finally it was solved by Professor Taylor, Principal of Aberdeen University, who had become interested in the preservation of *Am Fasgadh* and was able to arrange for the four Scottish universities to assume responsibility for it. Of course, I most gladly handed over the collection to them. I was sorry I had to charge them the cost of the house, but the capital that I should need for providing myself with somewhere else to live had been spent in buying it. I was offered the post of curator but I refused it. I wanted to make my home elsewhere. I had spent ten years at Kingussie running *Am Fasgadh* in the last of its three homes and it was 23 years since the idea of providing a shelter for homely Highland things first came to me. When I settled in Edinburgh in 1954 I was 67 and still able to lead a fairly active life. I hoped that I would find fellowship with those who worked professionally in the field in which my own interests lay and might even be of help by passing on what experience had taught me. In this I was disappointed; but I gained the much valued friendship of many private individuals who shared my interests either in remembering the old ways or wishing to learn about them and these friendships and the writing of books – especially *Highland Folk Ways* – have been a continued pleasure to me in my old age.

GLOSSARY

This selective list contains only those terms found in the text that may need explanation:

birlinn: a chief's barge in the Western Isles derived from the Norse word for a medieval longboat, *byrdingr*.

cabar lar: a type of spade used primarily for removing the upper layer of the soil or peat, prior to cultivation or peat cutting.

cas chrom: the crooked spade, implement of tillage peculiar to the Highlands, used for turning the ground where a plough cannot work.

coracle: a small oval rowing-boat made of skins or tarred or oiled canvas stretched on wickerwork or a wooden frame.

crotal: a lichen used for dying.

cruisie: an open iron lamp used with a rush wick.

deal: fir or pine board of standard size.

distaff: a stick-like implement used to hold combed wool which is fed on to a **spindle** (see below) for spinning into yarn.

dolly: a wooden shaft attached to a disk with projecting arms, used for beating and stirring clothes in a washing-tub.

eolith: a very early roughly-broken stone implement, or one naturally formed but assumed to have been used by man.

flail: an implement for threshing corn, consisting of a wooden bar (the swingle) hinged or tied to a handle.

goffering iron: an instrument used for ironing plaits or ruffles, especially in headgear such as a mutch.

iorram: a Gaelic boat-song.

in-field: one of the two main divisions of an arable farm of the eighteenth and early nineteenth centuries before the practice of crop rotation, consisting of the best land nearest the farm-buildings, kept continuously under crop and well manured with winter dung. More generally, the field or land lying nearest to the farm or homestead

lymphad: a Highland galley.

out-field: the earlier system of agriculture before enclosing and rotation of crops, the more out-lying and less fertile parts of a farm, in distinction to the **in-field** (see above).

peerman: a kind of candlestick used for holding aloft a smouldering fir-candle or sliver of resinous wood which provided light.

precentor: the leader of the singing of a church choir or congregation.

racan: instrument for breaking clods and used as a harrow.

ret: to rot by soaking or exposure to moisture.

séisach: a sofa or couch.

sidhe: fairy mound, realm beyond the senses.

skein: quantity of thread or yarn, wound to a certain length upon a reel, and usually put up in a kind of loose knot.

sowens: food made by fermenting the husks or bran of oats.

spindle: weighted device used to spin combed wool into yarn, often used in conjunction with distaff (see above).

tathing: manuring.